Old scarves, new trends

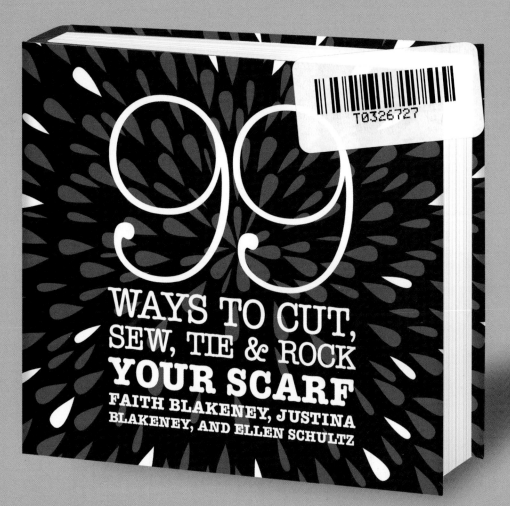

99 WAYS TO CUT, SEW, TIE & ROCK YOUR SCARF

FAITH BLAKENEY, JUSTINA BLAKENEY, AND ELLEN SCHULTZ

From a little design studio with a big vision comes a small book with lots of ideas! Simple techniques, household supplies, and a little imagination transform old scarves into new tops, ponchos, and party dresses. And every one of these 99 awe-inspiring projects takes an hour or less, from start to finish!

Potter CRAFT

compai.com
pottercraftnews.com

Craft:

Volume 07

transforming traditional crafts™

Special Section

SHOEWARE

Features

Columns

Vol. 07, April 2008. CRAFT (ISSN 1932-9121) is published 4 times a year by O'Reilly Media, Inc. in the months of January, April, July, and October. O'Reilly Media is located at 1005 Gravenstein Hwy. North, Sebastopol, CA 95472, (707) 827-7000. SUBSCRIPTIONS: Send all subscription requests to CRAFT, P.O. Box 17046, North Hollywood, CA 91615-9588 or subscribe online at craftzine.com/subscribe or via phone at (866) 368-5652 (U.S. and Canada), all other countries call (818) 487-2037. Subscriptions are available for $34.95 for 1 year (4 issues) in the United States; in Canada: $39.95 USD; all other countries: $49.95 USD. Application to Mail at Periodicals Postage Rates is Pending at Sebastopol, CA, and at additional mailing offices. POSTMASTER: Send address changes to CRAFT, P.O. Box 17046, North Hollywood, CA 91615-9588. Canada Post Publications Mail Agreement Number 41129568. Canada Postmaster: Send address changes to: O'Reilly Media, PO Box 456, Niagara Falls, ON L2E 6V2.

Bond with the Past

Craft:™ Projects

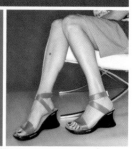

Our favorite *projects* are clothes you can make today, wear tonight.

Our favorite sewing *machine* is a Baby Lock.

As co-hosts of DIYStyle.net, we use our vodcasts to demonstrate fun and stylish projects that even a beginner can do.

We recommend Baby Lock for beginning sewers because you get so much more than a sewing machine. A Baby Lock retailer can be the next best thing to having your Mom teach you to sew (that's how we learned). They offer personal demonstrations to teach you the basics, and they're always available by phone if you get stuck. They even offer free lessons that help beginners sew better, faster.

So if wearing your own creations is an idea that appeals to you, check out a free demonstration at a Baby Lock retailer and get started.

Allyce king

Melissa Watson

Co-hosts,
DIYStyle.net

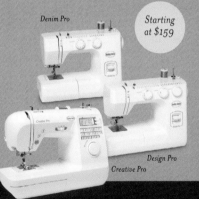

Denim Pro

Starting at $159

Design Pro

Creative Pro

www.babylock.com/designer

Call 800-422-2952 to find a retailer near you.

baby lock

FOR THE LOVE OF SEWING

Craft: Volume 07

Crafter Profiles

DIY

Make Cool Stuff

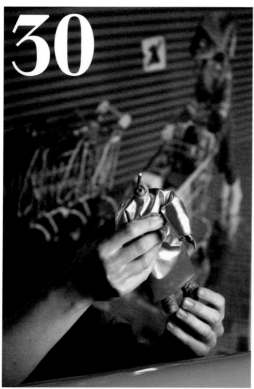

30

ON THE COVER

This pair of knitted high-tops by Katie Tesarowski is one of two Converse makeover projects in this issue. Learn to stitch up your own Chucks on page 52. Photographed by Garry McLeod and styled by Alex Murphy and Sam Murphy. Modeled by Natalie Zee Drieu and Lulu. Speaker illustration by Katie Wilson.

Craft:
transforming traditional crafts™

EDITOR AND PUBLISHER
Dale Dougherty
dale@oreilly.com

EDITORS-IN-CHIEF
Carla Sinclair
Tina Barseghian

CREATIVE DIRECTOR
Daniel Carter
dcarter@oreilly.com

MANAGING EDITOR
Shawn Connally
shawn@craftzine.com

DESIGNERS
Katie Wilson
Alison Kendall

ASSOCIATE MANAGING EDITOR
Goli Mohammadi
goli@craftzine.com

PRODUCTION DESIGNER
Gerry Arrington

SENIOR EDITOR
Natalie Zee Drieu
nat@craftzine.com

PHOTO EDITOR
Sam Murphy
smurphy@oreilly.com

COPY CHIEF
Keith Hammond

ASSOCIATE PUBLISHER
Dan Woods
dan@oreilly.com

ONLINE MANAGER
Terrie Miller

CIRCULATION DIRECTOR
Heather Harmon

STAFF EDITOR
Arwen O'Reilly

ACCOUNT MANAGER
Katie Dougherty
katie@oreilly.com

CONTRIBUTING EDITOR
Phillip Torrone

MARKETING & EVENTS COORDINATOR
Rob Bullington

CRAFT TECHNICAL ADVISORY BOARD
**Jill Bliss, Jenny Hart, Garth Johnson,
Leah Kramer, Alison Lewis, Matt Maranian,
Ulla-Maaria Mutanen, Kathreen Ricketson**

PUBLISHED BY O'REILLY MEDIA, INC.
Tim O'Reilly, CEO
Laura Baldwin, COO

Visit us online at craftzine.com
Comments may be sent to editor@craftzine.com

For advertising inquiries, contact:
Katie Dougherty, 707-827-7272, katie@oreilly.com

For Maker Faire and other event inquiries, contact:
Sherry Huss, 707-827-7074, sherry@oreilly.com

Contributing Artists:
Graziella Antonini, Melinda Beck, Damien Correll, Dustin Amery Hostetler, Brian Kaldorf, Anna Knott, Tim Lillis, Garry McLeod, Caroline Murphy, Brian Ulrich, Dan Videtich

Contributing Writers:
Mary Jane Anderson, Diane Baker, Susan Beal, Susie Bright, Annie Buckley, Cathy Callahan, Kathleen Conahan, Meredith Davey, Ivory Eileen, Ashley Jameson Eriksmoen, Meganne Fabrega, Diane Gilleland, Amy O'Neill Houck, Richard Humphrey, Melissa Kronenthal, Katie Kurtz, Thomas Maiorana, Teresa Mak, Matt Maranian, Rachel McConnell, Annie Mohaupt, Brookelynn Morris, Stephen L. Moss, Shannon Okey, Syuzi Pakhchyan, Charles Platt, Kristen Rask, Kathreen Ricketson, Wendy Seltzer, Annie Shao, Eve Oki Shirley, Eric Smillie, Luanne Teoh, Katie Tesarowski, Tiffany Threadgould, Wendy Tremayne, Tom Wyatt, Patricia Zapata

Interns: Matthew Dalton (engr.), Adrienne Foreman (web), Kris Magri (engr.), Lindsey North (crafts), Ed Troxell (edit.)

Customer Service cs@readerservices.craftzine.com
Manage your account online, including change of address at:
craftzine.com/account
866-368-5652 toll-free in U.S. and Canada
818-487-2037, 5 a.m.–5 p.m., Pacific

Contributors

 **Eve Oki Shirley** (*Baby Shoes Project*) loves seeing how things are made. When she couldn't figure out how shoes are made just by looking, she decided to find out. Eve loves traveling, finding knick-knacks from around the world, painting, filling coloring books, and shopping for tools and materials. Her favorite tool is a very sharp knife (for shoemaking, of course). She doesn't discriminate when it comes to colors or noodles, adoring all varieties of both. Last year, Eve relocated from Tokyo to Las Vegas with her husband.

Thomas Maiorana (*Open Source Shoes DIY*) began making shoes years ago when a roommate's cat peed in his favorite pair. Unable to replace them, he decided to make his own. He had so much fun that he's now committed to helping others do the same (bootyamor.org). In the world away from feet, Thomas works as a creative strategist and lives in San Francisco with his partner, Vida Mia, and their two cats, Zizou and Pema. They have yet to pee in his shoes.

 An eclectic crafter, **Mary Jane Anderson** (*Map Coffee Table Project*) is currently obsessed with spinning using a drop spindle (no wheel here!). If it weren't for her super-busy life and lack of superhero-strength wrists, she would spin every day. The only thing she loves more than crafting is her wonderful fiancé, Cal. Mary is a full-time student at Iowa State University and is excited to spend this summer in three different countries. She's currently working on a sweet Super Mario Brothers rug.

After living on the West Coast for eight years, **Meganne Fabrega** (*Travel Crafty: Amsterdam*) discovered her inner Yankee and now lives with her family in Portsmouth, N.H. When she's not haunting the stacks at the city library, she's baking desserts for her neighbors and exploring the mystery of thrummed mittens. Her work appears in the *San Francisco Chronicle*, *Publisher's Weekly*, and *Portsmouth Magazine*, in addition to other publications. She's currently working on her first novel.

 **Teresa Mak** (*Batik Project*) started making things as a way to be thrifty, learning from her parents, who immigrated to Canada 30 years ago. Her creativity spans genres, as she knits, makes soap, does ceramics, dyes textiles, cooks, and builds things around the house. She's so crafty that she's already created a red sweater pattern for her dream dog, Albert the dachshund (whom she doesn't actually have yet). Teresa relocated from Toronto to Hermosa Beach, Calif., where she lives in a beach house with her boyfriend and loves to take sunset walks on the beach. tallwheat.blogspot.com

Dustin Amery Hostetler (*Ergonomics Feature illustration*) has way too much up his sleeves and blames the internet for inspiring him to start new projects all the time. When he's not at work as special projects manager for threadless.com, he's busy publishing his art mag, *Faesthetic*, rehabbing a 100-year-old house, and frequenting antique stores. Dustin lives in Toledo, Ohio, with two really old cats named Pete and Tebro, a dog named Daphne, and his partner in crime and art, his wife, Jemma. His favorite food is salt, and you'll never find him without his pocketknife.

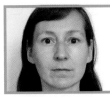 Photographer **Graziella Antonini** (*Becker-Echivard Profile photography*) was born in Italy, raised and trained in Switzerland, and is currently living and working in Paris. She's interested in many different fields of photography ranging from architecture to documentary to personal, in addition to video. For Graziella, the art of photography is "to be physically in one place while being mentally in another." graziellaantonini.com

Dale Dougherty
Welcome

>> Dale Dougherty is editor and publisher of MAKE and CRAFT magazines. dale@oreilly.com

The Cathedral and Bazaar Bizarre

"A great babbling bazaar of differing agendas" is how Eric S. Raymond describes the Linux software community in *The Cathedral and the Bazaar.* Raymond's book contrasts two different styles of organizing projects. The old style is like a cathedral: it originates from a unified plan that orders the work of highly specialized workers over several generations. When Raymond looked into the Linux project, he found a very different style: open, decentralized, some might say chaotic. He observed that building a cathedral required the design of an architect, while the bazaar model required a leader who was able to "recognize good design in others."

In the craft world, if the cathedral is Wal-Mart, then the alternative is Bazaar Bizarre.

Leah Kramer, a software developer from Boston, is one of the organizers of Bazaar Bizarre. Its original founders were about a dozen "arty types" who knew each other from local bands. Too familiar with typical holiday craft fairs that "smell like potpourri," they wondered what a craft fair might look like if it reflected their own tastes. What if they could find things they'd actually want to buy and give to friends?

Initially, they had a hard time finding enough crafters who represented what they were looking for — crafts that were clever, funny, or commenting on pop culture. They had to cajole friends into participating, some of whom had never crafted before.

Bazaar Bizarre got its start in 2001 with 20 exhibitors in a tiny VFW hall in Somerville, Mass. One of the first projects was macaroni glued on old album covers. "Craft is another way to express your style or your sense of humor," says Kramer. "It's about things you like, which could be TV shows, video games, or music."

Kramer attended the first Bazaar Bizarre and, seeing its potential, got involved the next year as an organizer. In its second year, Bazaar Bizarre had 100 vendors and 4,000 attendees. They had three times more applications than tables, so they put together a jury to select the best crafters. Eventually, Bazaar Bizarre would branch out to other cities, including Cleveland and Los Angeles, as well as becoming a part of Maker Faire in the Bay Area.

Kramer created craftster.org in 2003 using open source message-board software that she tweaked and tailored to fit her own ideas for the site. "People love to post how-to projects," says Kramer, comparing crafters to open source developers. "They enjoy the praise and recognition they get from sharing ideas, expertise, and designs." What they build over time is reputation in the community.

Not everyone wants to share, and nobody should be forced to do so, Kramer believes. "On Craftster," she adds, "we discourage people who sell what they make from posting their original project idea if they don't want people to copy it." However, the process of commercializing work can be difficult, whether selling crafts or software. People who are open sourcing or sharing their work are motivated to craft for different reasons.

"It doesn't matter so much what I sell. I just love to show off what I make," Kramer says. Many crafters do craft projects not as a job, she points out, but as something to do outside of work. "Crafting is a chance to exercise new skills and develop interests that you don't get to do at your day job."

In this issue, Tom Maiorana writes about platform shoes, or rather, shoes as an open source platform. He shows you how to disassemble shoes you already own and remake them in new ways. Modularity, he notes, is a key to success in open source projects because it makes projects easier to share. It means conceiving a project as a set of distinct components that can be worked on separately — failures in one module should not affect other modules — and then recombined in different ways.

By developing a platform for sharing, Bazaar Bizarre and Craftster are helping crafters expand their skills, having the kind of impact that open source has had among software developers. Having platforms for sharing helps to grow the community, not only in quantity, but in quality, as well. ✂

I was considering letting my subscription lapse, because I'm a boy and so many of the projects are too girly or too hard for me. But Volume 06 is great! Plenty of projects within my ability that don't threaten my fragile manhood. It convinced me to renew.

I liked the Quick Craft on bleaching shirts [*Volume 06, page 141*], but I have a better method that gives less, well, rough results. I make an outline with freezer paper and arrange words inside using wooden letters (a buck a letter at Target). The result is a shirt made ASAP that doesn't look like it was made ASAP. Here are some of the ones I've made.

—*Tom Carlson*

Thank you so much for the tutorial on embroidery and the various stitches [*Volume 06, page 135*]. I've always wanted to learn to embroider but have been too afraid to teach myself until now. I feel very inspired to go out and try it.

—*Kayleigh Arcari*

▣ Check out Dolin O'Shea's embroidery video tutorial at craftzine.com/06/101!

The hand-sewn free-range monsters are super cool. Thanks. Perfect thing to do while sick and stir-crazy. Attached is a picture of Flurge the Irked. He's not fierce or ferocious, just mildly peeved. And wait, here's Spilk, he's great too.

Actually, you all have created a monster-making monster.

—*Ellen Schinderman*

When I saw the cover for Volume 04, I totally fell in love with your magazine. I knew I had to have that scarf [*Volume 04, page 109*], so a month later I enrolled in a knitting course (it's the first pattern I've ever followed) and three months down the line, here it is — I made the finishing touches on Christmas Day. I knew the scarf would look fab but didn't realize it would be so warm and snuggly too, and although we never get snow in London, we do get a fierce wind, so I aim to wear it all season. Thanks.

—*Momtaz Begum-Hossain*

 Got something to say? Write to us at editor@craftzine.com.

Shoot. Edit. Print.

Practical Artistry
Learn how to apply the techniques and principles of classic photography so you can create great images with today's digital equipment.

Digital Photography Companion
Use these creative tips to take top-notch digital photos that reflect your artistic spirit.

Creative Digital Darkroom
Make your photographs shine with this clear, concise, insightful, and inspiring guide.

From capture to print, master the art of digital photography. O'Reilly digital photography books mentor you each step of the way as you reach your potential as an artist.

Buy 2 books, get 1 FREE!
Use offer code opc10 when you order directly from
O'Reilly at http://www.oreilly.com

O'REILLY®

Susie Bright
Susie's Home Ec

» Susie Bright is an amateur dressmaker and a professional writer. She blogs at susiebright.com.

Sewing Camp Confidential

None of us were eager to confess our vacation plans. We were vague with family and friends — "Oh, yes, seven days on the coast … sightseeing … you know" — even as we packed queen-size suitcases full of fabric and notions.

Civilians don't understand. We are the few, the proud — the nine women who signed up for a week-long, round-the-clock sewing workshop, hidden on the 10th floor of the Marines' Memorial Club in downtown San Francisco.

Our guru? Sandra Betzina, the legendary designer, teacher, and author who can sew, teach, create fashion, and write it all down with equal parts aplomb and grace. Every year she offers a series of seven-day sewing camps.

Each Christmas, as other friends talked about flying to Hawaii or surfing off the lip-of-whatever, I'd sigh, and whisper, "I wanna run away and go to sewing school."

Finally, I wrote the check and signed up. Reader, I was petrified. "I'm a mediocre seamstress! I don't know what to bring! I've never run a machine besides my own! I'm a fraud!"

But the real story behind my case of nerves was that I had never planned a vacation to do exactly what I pleased, to minister to my devotions. If you've ever discounted your passion for your craft and art, or said, "I never have time to sew anymore," then you know the kind of hole I'd been digging.

Our small class occupied a big meeting room of a grand postwar residential hotel and theater dedicated to Marine veterans. Betzina passed out her custom-made boxes of See's chocolates, and we sewed our asses off.

Every day (and night) was filled with working like elves on our own projects, taking in impromptu and planned "clinics" on special techniques and fabrics,

or trying on muslins in every single pattern size to discern our best fit. We took the dressmaker's tour of Chinatown. We ransacked a closet of garments Betzina had sewn so we could check out dozens of different designs on our figures. She measured each one of us, and drew "maps" of our basic alterations that we could apply to every pattern we work on.

Are you drooling yet?

I think Betzina realized early in her career that, as much as people might love to spend hours on a unique buttonhole, no one wants to soldier for days on a sewing project that they can't even pin over their chest in the end. Sewers are rightfully fearful that without "fit insurance," without the confidence that they've cut the cloth to make it right, it's demoralizing to make ill-fitting garments. The paper patterns you buy are only a general outline — they all have to be tailored to you. This is why so many people hide out in Home Dec, because every time they make something for their body, they end up crying in the mirror.

But as they say, knowledge is power. My mirror-shock days are over!

Let me use my own pattern alteration session with Betzina as an example. I already knew that I had to adjust patterns for my height, and to make a full-bust adjustment. I knew that pant patterns, which fit me in one spot, were disastrous in another.

Betzina showed me how both my bust curve and my tall-factor could be addressed by lengthening small amounts in three strategic places, instead of one big slash. She showed me how my upper chest needed a smaller adjustment where the sleeve meets the bodice, and drew a line on my paper sloper to show the way.

Many of us do desk work these days. Betzina points out how our work posture, and aging, lend us a bit of a hump in our upper back, just below the neck — ugh! It pulls your bodice out of shape, and

I have the wrinkles in all my dresses and blouses to prove it. She showed us how to alter our back pieces in that one small but critical area.

She demonstrated how to easily enlarge my cup size once I'd done all the other alterations first. Someday, I dream of being as relaxed as her — sewing and talking and drawing, all at the same time!

Finally, she showed me the "princess seam" technique for the rear of my pant leg, that makes me look like I'm ready for my celebrity close-up.

All of us have creative desire ... but instead of a competition, we pooled all our talents and treasures to a tremendous effect.

As you can imagine, all the students had different figures, and it was fascinating to see how she worked with each person's silhouette.

I picked out the prettiest fabrics in my suitcase to work with. They happened to be the most difficult: tie-dyed transparent silk georgette with an embroidered border — shoot me now! — and a lavender loose-weave sweater knit that would sooner smother me than go easy.

But with a class like this, you have the time to master these demons. After our class marathon, I can sew French seams like a soldier can strip a rifle in the dark. I can make idiot-proof tailor's tacks with waxed basting thread. I mitered my mighty collar points; I steamed invisible melting stabilizers onto knits and purls. I curved a neckline over a breast so that no gap could ever be seen. I am invincible! I laugh in the face of Viking sergers!

Sorry, the Marines got me a little worked up.

I did turn out to be the most inexperienced sewer in this class, although they've seen greener virgins than me. But instead of my ghastly premonitions coming true, everyone in class was thrilled for me and my little "breakthroughs." I had the pleasure of being with a whole group of women who are as crazy about sewing as I am, the ultimate nest. All of us have creative desire, the kind of drive you see on *Project Runway* shows. But instead of a competition, we pooled all our talents and treasures to a tremendous effect.

Sewing classes are not inexpensive, for they are a luxury of time and personal attention. I'm reminded of one of my sewing author heroes, John Giordano, who once advised, in his chapter "10 Ways to Save for the Sewing Machine That You Want": "Sell your blood."

Yes, sometimes you have to break on through to the other side. Runway hostess Heidi Klum may enjoy her little "What were they thinking?" critiques. But I stopped just thinking about it, just watching other people do what I'd always dreamed of. Doing it, and holding the results in my needle-hot hands, is truly the best. ✄

Hands On: The San Francisco Sewing Experience:
sandrabetzina.com/experience.htm

Idiot-proof tailor's tacks:
craftzine.com/go/ttacks

The Sewing Machine Guide by John Giordano:
craftzine.com/go/giordano

Illustration by Melinda Beck

Penciled In

Photography by Dean Powell

Inspired by the beautiful but dangerous sea urchin, as well as by repeating patterns in nature, **Jennifer Maestre** has created a powerful body of work from the most ordinary of materials: nails and pencils.

A onetime type designer, Maestre went back to school to get a fine art degree in her 30s. "I became obsessed with trying to make sea urchins, using nails and window screen. Eventually, I started making larger and larger pieces, because I fell in love with the textures created by the masses of nails," she remembers. When she became frustrated by limitations, she had a breakthrough.

Cutting pencils into 1-inch lengths, she drilled a tiny hole in each section, turning the pencil piece into a bead. Using peyote stitch, a common beading technique that lends itself to sculpture, she was able to create forms with incredible texture.

The shapes are organic from afar, but humorously familiar up close, as you realize that the surface is made up of hundreds of sharp pencil points.

Maestre's sculptures undulate and seethe, bearing names like *Asteridae,* a botanical subclass; *Chimera,*

referring to an ancient Greek monster made up of many parts; and *Silkie,* a mythological creature that transforms from seal to human and back again.

Where do her names come from? "I feel like my sculptures can't go off into the world without names, so I try and find ones that fit," she says from her Concord, Mass., home. "Sometimes it takes as long to name them as to make them, but sometimes I know the name from the first stitch."

When she needs a break, Maestre has a few other projects on a back burner; she also creates colorful (and glossily smooth) jewelry from pencil cross-sections, as well as beaded sculptures.

"If I'm having a bad day sharpening pencils, I can put down the sharpener and go make pins," she admits. But pencils still hold her attention for now. The added benefit? "I hear some great pencil stories!"
—*Arwen O'Reilly*

➤➤ **Jennifer Maestre's Sculptures:** jennifermaestre.com

Felted Bear Hugs

It isn't easy to categorize the lush, felted works of San Francisco-based artist **James Gobel**, but they fall somewhere between quilting, painting, and mosaic. To complicate matters, Gobel's art is at once masculine and feminine, homey and theoretical, high art and grounded craft.

Made primarily with felt, yarn, and paint, his work has a relaxed sensibility that belies his meticulous process. In homage to "bears," a subculture of gay male identity, each image features a large man — or two — blessed with the smooth grace of royalty and a rosy glow. Though the hefty men lounge in elegant repose or concentrate earnestly, Gobel's guys aren't the stuff of slick fashion spreads. Rather than skinny jeans or designer suits, they don flannel shirts and suspenders, John Deere tees and jeans, at peace with their big bellies and broad faces.

While crafting a fresh image for big men, Gobel has also created a unique process for making fabric-based paintings. Starting with a photograph, he transforms it into a drawing on canvas and then carefully glues yarn over the drawn lines, effectively sketching with string. He traces the negative spaces between lines to make detailed templates, and then cuts shapes from either wool or acrylic felt. Gobel doesn't sew pieces to the canvas, but rather glues each one in place before painting in details (yes, that's glued felt in the image above). More recently, he's taken to embroidering for added specificity.

Gobel, an associate professor at California College of the Arts, has shown his works in many exhibitions, including the Hammer Museum in Los Angeles and the Kravets/Wehby Gallery in New York.

He concedes that "some people are startled by the nature of the subject matter," and while he recognizes his work's role in helping to change attitudes and subvert stereotypes, Gobel isn't preaching so much as adoring. He likes his characters and the way they look; the colorful tapestries, he says, make fat men "seem more approachable, or irresistible, because they have this look like a cuddly bear."

—Annie Buckley

>> **James Gobel's Felt Art: marxzav.com**

Photograph courtesy of James Gobel

Fenced In, Kept Out

The politics of **Lacey Jane Roberts'** sculpture *We couldn't get in. We couldn't get out.* may seem obvious at first. Her classic chain-link and concertina wire structure automatically begs the question of any fence: who or what is being kept out?

But this fence's sculptural presence is about another kind of barrier. "Physical boundaries are a lot less scary than the invisible boundaries we stay within in order to control ourselves and control others," Roberts says.

Prior to embarking on what turned out to be a yearlong project, this San Francisco resident created hand-knit artwork that explored less obvious boundaries, specifically those relating to gender and queerness.

Her 10-foot-high by 20-foot-long fence is a more overt statement, with its exaggerated features leaning toward campy. Its amplified use of pink is Roberts' commentary on culturally prescribed femininity, while its overall comic effect undermines the typically serious purpose of fences.

To make the fence, Roberts and a crew of her friends hand-cranked more than 300 skeins of yarn on a 1970s Mattel Barbie Knit Magic and other children's knitting machines ordered online. The resulting strands of 15-foot-long yarn tubes were threaded with wire to form the zigzagging fence pattern. "I wanted to over-perform the craft element in order to emphasize that it's entirely handmade," the artist explains.

Since every border is read in context — whether it's the Berlin Wall, Israel and Palestine, or the U.S.-Mexican border — the artist was curious to see if people would trespass against a floppy, neon-pink fence. Most people did not even ask to pass — not even in cars. At an art opening, people had conversations through the fence, "which was really creepy."

Roberts installed it in San Francisco's famed, mural-filled Clarion Alley, where it stayed for a day. "What side of the fence is important?" she wonders. It depends on who built it.

—*Katie Kurtz*

>> **Boundary-Busting Knitting: laceyjaneroberts.com**

Jonesy Town

Sam "Jonesy" Goldstein is a very busy young man. When not going to school, writing scripts, playing the guitar, or stenciling tees for a local clothing boutique, this 15-year-old's making new friends. Friends made of socks.

His Sockyfellers came into being about two years ago, after Goldstein saw another artist's sock creations. "I had seen a lot of the new art/toy stuff that was happening. It really inspired me to make my own weird things," he explains. Sewing them up isn't a problem since Goldstein's been "vaguely" sewing since he was 6 years old. He incorporates chopsticks as the basis for antlers and buttons for eyes. Often, the sock heels become lips.

Goldstein says his creation process involves the admittedly clichéd act of setting the object free, the way Michelangelo described carving sculptures. "There's already some form in the marble (or sock). I just set it free."

Naming his creations follows a similar path. "By the time I'm done, they already kind of have personalities, so I just name them whatever seems appropriate," he explains. "Or I just make up something crazy. That works, too." To date, Samantha, Scrampy, and Skip are among those set free.

Not one to think about the future ("Maybe that's why I make stuffed animals!"), when pressed Goldstein thinks he'll pursue a career in graphic design or some other type of art. "I'm really not sure yet exactly, but it will definitely involve art," he says.

Although his hand-stenciled T-shirts are selling well in an Austin shop, Goldstein hasn't been able to bring himself to sell any of his Sockyfeller pals. He hopes to be able to soon. His stencil designs favor punk and rock figures — Bob Dylan, Joe Strummer, The Ramones, Lou Reed. But Karl Marx and zombies make guest appearances.

"They're selling pretty well. Since I have to do school and everything I haven't been able to replenish the stock as much as I would like. School seems to get in my way a lot, actually …" —*Shawn Connally*

≫ **Jonesy's Art:** jonesypop.com, craftzine.com/07/handmade_sock

Photograph by Sam Murphy

Photograph by Natalie Trujillo

Against the Grain

I've known **Natalie Trujillo** since third grade, so I know a lot about her. Like that time in high school when she got drunk and threw up in the back seat of Missy Karabian's brand-new Corvette.

Now she's all grown up and doesn't have time for such nonsense, because she's too busy in her Oakland, Calif., workshop carving wonderful things out of wood.

A graduate of California College of the Arts ("When I went there it was called California College of Arts and Crafts — and I never saw anything wrong with that!" she asserts), Trujillo uses everything from fallen branches scavenged from the sidewalk during municipal tree trimming ("domestic hardwoods," as she likes to classify them), to exotic ebony nabbed from the scrap piles of fellow woodworkers.

A whittler from early on, Trujillo carved her first ring for herself. People noticed, friends made requests, and soon after, she took a booth at a craft fair and sold out the first day.

These days Trujillo's work is hotter than a California wildfire with a strong wind: featured in the *San Francisco Chronicle* and picked up by several Bay Area galleries, her pieces are now selling as far south as Los Angeles, and as far east as Brattleboro, Vt. The rings are so well received that she's now moved on to bracelets and cuff links, tearing through wood so fast she makes the most voracious colony of carpenter ants look like rogue amateurs.

Trujillo makes it look easy. She'll facet some of her pieces like the large jewels on cocktail rings, or crown them by taking advantage of a complex and densely textured bark. She delights in a grain's subtleties and imperfections, celebrating them with perfect placement among the carving, and creating additional dimension with a rubbing of organic food-grade linseed oil and a rich polish.

So if you're lookin' to dress up your digits with one of Trujillo's signature timbered baubles, get in line. But bypass any desire to make a Natalie Wood joke — and don't take her for a spin in your new Corvette.
—*Matt Maranian*

>> **For more info:** nt.rings@gmail.com

Plastic Herb Planters

Do you have a pile of plastic containers you never use? Put them to work by creating an herb garden paradise. It's a great way to recycle your plastic, plus it puts fresh herbs at your fingertips.

You will need: Plastic containers, plastic lids to fit under containers, power drill, ¼" to ½" drill bit, scrap piece of wood, rocks, potting soil, herb seeds or plants

1. Select containers.

Containers that work best are ones that are solid in color. Clear and translucent containers can grow mold inside, so it's best to stay away from those. Choose a lid for each container that fits comfortably under the base. This will collect water overflow.

✳ TIP: We used all the scrap plastic we could get our hands on for this project: food storage containers, a Frisbee, a small bucket, even a plastic piggy bank. You'll be surprised at the plastic scrap you can dig up once you start looking.

2. Drill a water drainage hole.

Place the scrap wood on a flat surface and center the bottom of your container on the wood. Drill a hole in the bottom center of the container. Make sure that the plastic is flush against the wood, otherwise the plastic can bend and crack.

3. Get your container plant-ready.

Place several medium-sized rocks in the bottom of the container. This will help the water drain through the pot. Fill the rest of the container with potting soil until it reaches about ½" from the top. Place the container atop the lid.

4. Plant your seeds.

Put your seeds or plants into the soil, give them a watering, and then sit back and watch them grow.

Tiffany Threadgould is the author of *This into That* books and runs a crafty recycle business, RePlayGround. replayground.com

Photography by Tiffany Threadgould

Maker Faire ®

Meet the Makers

Build.
Craft.
Hack.
Play.
Make.

SF BAY AREA May 3 & 4, 2008
SAN MATEO FAIRGROUNDS

AUSTIN October 18 & 19, 2008
TRAVIS COUNTY EXPO CENTER

FEATURING: Austin Children's Museum, Austin Green Art, Edible Austin, MAKE & CRAFT Labs, Bazaar Bizarre, and more!

MakerFaire.com

OUR FAVORITE TRINKETS & TREASURES

1. Bee Mine
You have to hold your breath when looking at this tiny, perfect paper bee. Elsa Mora carefully creates her paper sculptures layer by layer, capturing the concrete beauty of the world as well as the metaphysical nature of art.
elsita.etsy.com

2. Play with Fire
Laura Lobdell's clever jewelry elevates the ordinary objects in our lives to precious keepsakes. A slender gold matchstick comes in a daring red matchbook that proclaims "I play with fire"; popcorn bursts from a ring like kinetic diamonds.
lauralobdell.com

3. Crochet Vase
Crafter and stylist Paul Lowe created this beautiful crochet-wrapped vase. The antique look of the crochet is surprisingly modern when holding water.
sweetpaul.
typepad.com

Photograph of crochet vase by Frances Janisch

4. Childhood Heroes

Doodle stitching author Aimee Ray embroidered her childhood heroes. We love Bob Ross and his "happy little trees," and who among us didn't long for Crystal Gayle's beautiful hair? The technique is simple and reminiscent of childhood; the sentiment is anything but. dreamfollow.com

5. Tea for Time

If you've ever saved a precious but broken teapot, you'll relish these. British product designer Christine Misiak transforms thrift-store tea sets, with eclectically mismatched handles and a new coat of bright lacquer, into wholly desirable objects. christine misiak.co.uk

6. Lanyard Lamps

Kevin Patrick McCarthy's lanyard and monofilament lampshades give new meaning to that summer camp staple, opening up new possibilities of texture, light, and shape. kevinpatrick mccarthy.com

IF THE SHOE FITS ...

Here's a collection of shoes that make us gasp, blink, and drool. Ever since we decided on a "shoe" theme for this issue, the editorial inboxes have been filling up with high heels, sneakers, and booties that make our hearts race. Some are conceptual projects, some belong in galleries, and others are deliciously wearable.

📷 *See our online gallery at craftzine.com/07/curio for more fab shoes!*

This wallpaper is part meditation on the "shape and shadow" of shoes, and part hopeful replacement for consumerism.
lisabengtsson.se

1

2

1. Knit Sneakers
Sweetly clunky, Nina Braun's sculptures are a nod to nostalgia and the sweatshops behind the shoes.
ninabraun.net/work/sneakers

2. For the Birds
Our avian friends like these birdseed-covered shoes, from German designer Aart van Bezooyen, almost as much as we do!
materialstories.com

3

3. Red Hot
With her ravishing scarlet heels, Finnish shoe designer Minna Parikka proves that all is not cold close to the Arctic Circle.
minnaparikka.com

4. Street Sneak

A collab project between REVISE CMW and ST!ZO from Chitown (*see Volume 04's graffiti DIY*), they're painted with mad skills. craftzine.com/go/poison

5. Paint

Ndeur Shoes rescues vintage heels from propriety and gives them a funky edge. Don't worry, these fit right in at the office. ndeurshoes.etsy.com

6. Sweet Feet

Built for giants with a sweet tooth, artist Andy Yoder's shoes are made from licorice, making comfort shoes a feast for the eyes, too. andyyoder.com

7. Très Chic

This clever and elegant design takes a flat sheet of cut felt and folds it to become a pair of baby booties like no others. studio.lo.neuf.fr/objets.html

8. Pac Man

Argentine street style meets 80s video art with these painted shoes. flickr.com/photos/thekalaka

CRAFTER

SEWING FOR JOY

BY STEPHEN L. MOSS

Danny Mansmith makes his world one scrap at a time.

"Bad sewing is a really big inspiration to me," says Chicago fiber artist Danny Mansmith, 36, who creates clothing, accessories, soft sculpture, and drawings in his Northwest Side studio.

"I walk into a thrift store and see a garment made by hand that's really badly made. I think 'They didn't know what they were doing, but they still needed to make this.' That sort of fire, that's what it's all about for me."

Much of Mansmith's work incorporates fabric scraps, wooden trinkets, found objects like ticket stubs, and old photographs. "My grandma was one of my biggest influences. She was a big dumpster diver. She worked as a housekeeper in the wealthy neighborhoods, and sometimes I would help her out. After her shift was over we would walk the alleys, finding things the rich people had thrown away. She would find a chair and reupholster it herself. She would find a frame in the garbage and make a picture to go in it. Her whole house was all found and made things."

Mansmith, the sensitive redhead who was picked on in school, felt shunned by mainstream society. Inspired by fiber-artist friends, he decided to create his own wardrobe as an expression of his identity. "I bought the cheapest sewing machine I could find and immediately started taking apart all my clothes and following the patterns. I think I burned through that first machine in about a month."

Eschewing classes and how-to books, Mansmith learned his art by studying the homemade and vintage clothes he found in thrift stores. "I wanted to make my work look sort of haphazard and naïve, with flaws, but still be well made," he says. "It took me most of the 90s to figure out how to do that."

Mansmith began showing his work in 1999 and opened his own studio in 2005. "It's a balancing act," he says of making his art a business. "I do this because it's my joy. But I have to figure out a way to make some money and feed myself."

He sells his work on Etsy, and has shown in galleries from New York to Florida. He was recently chosen to design custom panels for design giant Herman Miller's 2007 Neocon display. "I rarely find myself with nothing to do these days," he says.

Mansmith calls his process "improvisational" and champions a jump-first-ask-questions-later attitude. "Don't say, 'Oh, I can't do this because I don't have money to buy the right paintbrush or the right canvas.' When I started painting I didn't have a canvas, so I took the labels off soup cans, gessoed them together, and painted on that."

Mansmith doesn't agonize over the details of his materials or his process, or spend time worrying about what the rest of the fiber art world is doing. "I just make things that make me happy." ✂

➕ See more of Mansmith's work at
scrap-dannymansmith.squarespace.com.

Stephen L. Moss tunes pianos, fixes harps, and writes about interesting stuff from his home in Milwaukee, Wis.

Photograph by Anna Knott

FIBER IMPROV: Danny Mansmith at play in his Chicago studio.

CRAFTER

FIN ART

BY ERIC SMILLIE

Anne-Catherine Becker-Echivard is hooked on the drama of the diorama.

Most artists would struggle to get good face from a fish. But French photographer and stage designer Anne-Catherine Becker-Echivard lands trophy shots as easily as her gilled buddies breathe water. "I play the stage manager," she says coyly. "It's totally natural for me."

That's probably because Becker-Echivard and fish go way back, to childhood vacations spent in the village of Pirou, on the Normandy coast. There, she explains, "I learned to catch them, to stack them in racks, to scale and clean them on the boat, and to smoke them myself. My brother and I played with them like dolls. I loved to have a sardine or a mackerel in my pocket."

Youthful games became a full-blown obsession in 1997 when, at age 26, Becker-Echivard took nine months of instruction in documentary photography and began shooting elaborate scenes starring piscine protagonists. The scenarios can be over 6 feet long and take months to prepare, using wood, cardboard, paint, and other materials you might find in a set-design studio. For the characters, she fits fresh fish heads onto plastic doll bodies or wire forms. Her mother sews the costumes, turning the whole production into a family enterprise.

Only the best specimens will do. "The eyes are very important in the picture, and they must be dark," she explains. She usually shops at Rungis, the world's largest wholesale produce market, or at her local store in Paris' Chinatown, the 13th Arrondissement. She has a soft spot for the sea bass' facial structure

and serious air, and the whiting's naïve and friendly looks, but she employs many varieties, depending on the characters and the atmosphere she wants her final picture to evoke. Once they're cast, she pampers her actors with wet paper during the shoot, which can last a whole day. "It's hot under the spotlights, so I just take care that my lead doesn't get cooked before he gets his chance at fame," she says dotingly.

All of this careful crafting, however, goes on behind the scenes. At the end of a shoot, she throws away the props. The public sees only the final product: large, dramatic prints swimming with commentary on human affairs (acbe.eu). "It's like backstage at the theater," she explains. "People are impressed when they learn that it's all handmade, but the real setup is much less impressive, much less dreamlike."

As for Becker-Echivard's stars, the camaraderie goes only so far. "The fish also have to be fresh," she adds, "because I eat them afterwards. If I have a lot, I even organize a big dinner with friends and family." She likes to cook them on an open flame, "with just olive oil, herbes de Provence, lemon, salt, and pepper. Or in my favorite dish, bouillabaisse."

As part of the festivities, Becker-Echivard takes each guest in turn and points out exactly which character he or she is eating. While some may consider this a bit unappetizing, others might call it tasteful art. ✂

Eric Smillie is a freelance writer living in Oakland, Calif.

Photography by Graziella Antonini and Anne-Catherine Becker-Echivard (bottom)

⭐ **PISCINE SCENE:**
(top to bottom)
Becker-Echivard
takes a break on
set; the artist outfits
her models and
prepares them for
costume check;
things get hopping
in her photograph
Made in China.

📷 See more of her
work at acbe.eu.

Travel Crafty

AMSTERDAM

BY MEGANNE FABREGA

Wander the Dutch metropolis for craft-related treasures.

A msterdam isn't all canals and bicycles! The city has lots of stores, galleries, markets, and museums that cater to a crafter's every whim. Don't forget to pack your walking shoes — this city is best explored on foot to appreciate its irresistible charm.

Noordermarkt

Corner of Westerstraat and Lijnbaansgracht
Mondays 9 a.m.–1 p.m.

When planning your trip to Amsterdam, be sure to schedule it around this must-see open market. Stalls are bursting at the seams with bolts of fabric from plain cotton to vibrant silks, plus buttons, notions, trims, tassels, and any other sewing materials a crafter could ever need. At the end of the market, the fun continues with a flea market featuring lots of vintage clothes, as well as crafters like Stoffen en Sloffen (stoffenensloffen.nl), who sell vintage aprons, handmade bags, and hard-to-find bedding from the 60s and 70s. Be prepared to fight the crowd to get your one-of-a-kind bag.

Food Match: Head on over to Café 't Smalle on the corner of Egelantiersgracht and Prinsengracht for a canal view and some *appeltaart mit slagroom* (apple cake with whipped cream).

Photography by Meganne Fabrega

Meganne Fabrega is a freelance writer and knitter in Portsmouth, N.H. Her work has appeared in *Publisher's Weekly* and the *San Francisco Chronicle*.

De Afstap
Oude Leliestraat 12 afstap.nl

According to the knitters that meet at Café de Jaaren every Monday night, De Afstap is the place for all things yarn in Amsterdam. From Rowan Biggy to oh-so-soft Cashcotton, your biggest problem will be choosing your favorite color. If needlepoint calls your name, they've got that covered, with a back room of threads from floor to ceiling, and a loft of patterns galore.

Food Match: Is there such a thing as cheese heaven? Find out at De Kaaskamer (Runstraat 7), which sells more than 300 types of cheese from all over Europe. Perfect picnic time!

Coppenhagen Kralen
Rozengracht 54 coppenhagenbeads.nl

Niko and Hillian Coppenhagen may have a shop packed with every bead under the sun, but for them quality takes precedence over quantity: they hand-pick every bead. More than 90% are made of glass; other materials include bone, shell, and wood. Niko is the third generation to run Holland's first bead shop, and takes pride in his rare and antique pieces. From itty-bitty Buddhas to Delft-inspired orbs, this is the place for any serious beader.

Food Match: In Holland, it's all about the *pannenkoeken*. So choose from more than 30 varieties at Pancakes! Amsterdam at Berenstraat 38 (pancakesamsterdam.nl).

Dam Square Souvenirs
Dam 17 dutchsouvenirs.com

All the tourist shops are selling bright yellow clogs, so why not buy a pair of unfinished clogs and glam them up yourself? Make your way through the miniature ceramic tchotchkes in typical Dutch Delft blue to find the largest selection of unfinished clogs in Amsterdam. A hot glue gun, paint, and sequins, and you've made yourself a one-of-a-kind pair! You can't miss this shop in the heart of the city — just look for the giant yellow clog.

Food Match: The cakes at De Taart van M'n Tante (Ferdinand Bolstraat 10, detaart.com) will inspire you to get out the marzipan and start sculpting your own masterpieces. Enjoy a slice of *zweedsetaart* (a cream-filled almond tart).

Craft
WITH CAUTION

BY KRISTEN RASK

A few preventative steps can help ward off injury.

Most of us have experienced "the zone." We're deep into knitting, sewing, or otherwise creating our masterpiece, and nothing will stop us from forging ahead. We don't hear the phone ringing! We don't have time to go to the bathroom! And that's why we love our craft: it allows us to block out the world.

But although it's meant to relax us, crafting can start to take a toll on our bodies. If we don't take the necessary precautions, we can suddenly find ourselves in serious pain. But here's the good news: making small changes to your crafting routine and to your tools can prevent a lot of unnecessary suffering.

After consulting a few avid crafters, we've compiled a list of tips to help you help yourself. Some of these may sound intuitive, but unless you take heed, you won't reap the benefits.

1. REFASHION YOUR TOOLS

Working for hours at a time with small tools will invariably wreak havoc on your hands, wrists, and arms. Avoid tendonitis at all costs, warns Susie Ghahremani, a San Diego-based artist who creates small-scale paintings and crafts. After years of working with narrow tools, Ghahremani sought professional help from an occupational therapist who is helping to retrain her muscles. To avoid further damage, Ghahremani wrapped sports grip tape around her brushes to add width, making them easier to hold.

Likewise, Seattle-based needle-felter Moxie, who suffers from arthritis, has developed her own ergonomic needle-felting tools, which she sells on her site by special request. You'll find a litany of websites selling ergonomic crafting tools that offer a wider range of motion.

2. WEAR PROTECTIVE GEAR

Crafters who work with felt, like Seattle-based Candi Hibert, may notice tightness in their chests, watery eyes, itchy skin, and allergies.

"After working with wool felt for the past couple of years, I've noticed just recently that I've become extra sensitive to the material," she says. "After hours of sewing, my eyes get red and irritated, I get wheezy, and I get an itchy, bumpy rash on my face and arms."

To prevent these symptoms, Hibert started wearing a dust mask to protect herself from fibers floating throughout her studio. And to avoid getting tiny wool fibers stuck to her eyelashes, she's switched to wearing her prescription eyeglasses instead of her contact lenses.

"This way, my eyes are protected, and I don't end the night looking like I had a hard night of partying," she says.

3. TAKE A BREAK AND STRETCH

This might be old news to you, but it can't be repeated enough. Put your work down and walk away for a few minutes at regular intervals. Your body needs this time to recoup so you can go back with renewed energy and relaxed muscles.

Take advantage of the natural pauses that come up while you're crafting, says Melissa Alvarado, part owner of Stitch Lounge, a San Francisco studio that offers sewers tools, advice, and resources.

Sewers, for example, inevitably run out of thread, and must get up to rethread the bobbin. That's the perfect time to take a stretch. Set an alarm for every half-hour or hour, then stand up and walk around the room, stretching out your arms and back.

Elizabeth Rainey, a Seattle-based yoga instructor, offers this suggestion: bend your body at 90° and place both hands against the wall at the same height as your hips. You can bend your knees or keep them straight, but keep your hands level with your hips. This will open up your shoulders while stretching your back and neck.

4. WATCH YOUR BACK

If you're sitting on a chair or sofa for hours at a time, always have lumbar support while you craft. Put a small pillow against your lower back to help keep your spine straight, says Michael Swenson, an occupational therapist in Seattle.

Also, keep both your feet on the ground while you work. "Your legs are made up of a closed chain of bones and muscles," he says. "Starting out with balance and support beneath your feet will ultimately carry balance up through your pelvis and into your whole upper body." Good posture is also important in minimizing symptoms of repetitive strain injury, he adds.

For those spending a lot of time on their feet, like Marie Kare, founder of the Sampler, a San Francisco-based mail-order company selling handcrafted goods, flip-flops are not going to fly as supportive footwear. Kare invested in a pair of MBT ergonomic shoes, and placed a soft rubber mat on her floor, which softened the impact of standing for hours on end.

5. SWITCH IT UP

Mastering one craft is great, but for us dabblers, it's good news to hear the importance of shifting from one craft to another. If you're working on sewing a dress and you really want to finish that knitted scarf for your best friend's birthday, switch back and forth every couple of hours. This will help you take breaks and will allow your body to engage in a variety of movements.

For Portland, Ore.-based artist Jill Bliss, who makes everything from earrings to stationery and runs a business selling her goods, the problems evolved over time. It started with pain in her hands, which then spread to her shoulders and now her lower back. She's developed sciatica and has sought help from a physical therapist and a chiropractor.

But Bliss knows she has some control over her environment. At any given time, she has three projects going on simultaneously so that she can alternate between them.

Like Kare, she also invested in a pair of MBT shoes for days spent standing. And lastly, she works shorter hours spread out throughout the entire week, which spreads the amount of concentrated work time, allowing for more frequent breaks.

Our bodies can take a lot of stress, but when your body starts complaining, don't forget to listen!

Kristen Rask owns a small store in downtown Seattle called Schmancy. Her book *Plush You! Lovable Misfit Toys to Sew and Stuff* is based on an annual show she has at the store. She loves to make stuff in any spare moment she can get. schmancytoys.com

Artistic LICENSE

BY WENDY SELTZER

How to negotiate the line between trademark infringement and your First Amendment rights.

If you use recognizable brands in your art, does that make you a budding Warhol or just a juicy lawsuit target? While you might get a cease-and-desist letter invoking trademark or publicity law, in fact the law is often on your side.

When referencing or riffing upon subjects of pop culture, crafters may be accused of violating a company's *trademark* or a celebrity's *right of publicity*. Can a company stop us from leaving its logo on our recycled crafts? When we mock products or depict celebrities who parade their lives before us, are we infringing their rights?

In many cases the answer is no, as most trademark and publicity restrictions apply only against exploitation "in commerce." But when it comes to work prepared for sale, it's wise to keep in mind some guidelines that can help smooth the way.

TRADEMARK

When someone becomes known for their products or services, trademark law shields their *source-identifying name and logos* against uses likely to confuse buyers. Trademark is designed to protect the consumer by giving manufacturers the right to stop the *misleading* commercial use of their identities. I can't pass off fizzy water as Coca-Cola to lure thirsty buyers, or impersonate one of Etsy's hotshot artists if I'm just getting started — I have to establish my own name and reputation.

That doesn't mean that all uses of trademarks are off-limits. The "*likelihood of confusion*" standard protects those who use others' trademarks in ways that don't confuse the consumer: the author whose fictional characters wear real-world fashions; the

artist who includes real product labels in a collage; the stitcher who crafts a "Chewy Vuitton" dog toy. These users and their crafts pass muster because they *don't imply sponsorship or endorsement* from the trademark holder.

More specifically, you can use trademarks to *refer to trademarked items* that the marks identify. If you're knitting up a sock to keep your music player safe, you don't need Apple's permission to describe it as an "iPod cozy." Although you shouldn't emblazon the Apple logo on your web storefront unless you have a license from Apple, you're free to use the marks as necessary to convey your product's compatibility. Likewise, for all the NFL's bluster, you can invite friends to a Super Bowl party without being forced into circumlocutions like "the big game."

In a logo-filled world, branded products may also be the raw materials for recycled crafts. Target recently threatened Timbuk2, a maker of messenger bags that commissions artists to create designs and allows consumers to make their own, when the red-and-white bull's-eye popped up on bags made from recycled plastic. Target complained that the use "could give the impression that these bags originate from, are somehow sponsored by, or are otherwise affiliated with Target."

If you're crafting for yourself or as a gift, you don't have those commercial worries. But if you're selling your work, you should make it clear to buyers and viewers that your work is *independent* craft, averting confusion. Though Timbuk2 chose to pull the bags, it's far from clear that they were obliged. You don't need permission from every brewery to make a bottle-cap purse, so long as you don't claim it's a "Bud."

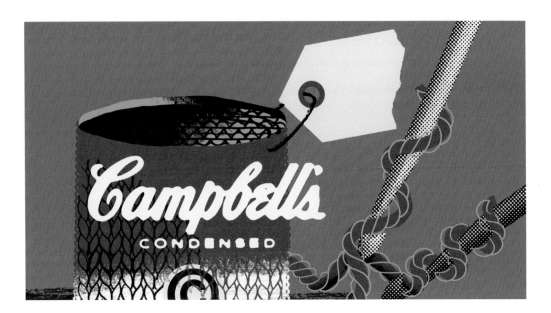

Like basic copyright, the core of trademark law strikes a reasonable balance. But trademark too is being pushed out of its equilibrium. Federal law has recently expanded to prohibit *"dilution," or uses that weaken the distinctiveness of famous marks*, even if no one is confused. So everyone wants to be "famous," and brand owners often claim that even parody or critical references dilute their brands, as when Mutual of Omaha chased down anti-nuclear

> *The First Amendment is part of our protections: where trademarks are part of our surroundings, we're not forced to shutter our cameras or censor our speech.*

protesters with "Mutant of Omaha" T-shirts. But federal law is clear that noncommercial uses cannot dilute. And trademark hasn't all gone to the dogs. The makers of Chewy Vuitton munchable handbag-toys and Timmy Holedigger dog cologne both managed to shake the infringement and dilution claims made against them.

PUBLICITY

Celebrities are part of the cultural conversation of craft, too. If your commercial crafting depicts recognizable people, you might have to contend with the right of publicity, a trademark-like right to control commercialization of celebrities' names and images. Like trademark, this right is countered by our First Amendment rights to talk about our culture. Courts have struck the balance by trying to determine whether a use is *artistically transformative* (good) or merely *exploitative* (not good).

It's not always a clear call: silk-screened Three Stooges T-shirts were deemed insufficiently transformative in California, while lithograph prints of Tiger Woods poised mid-swing at the Masters Tournament in Augusta, Ga., were protected as "artistic" in Ohio. If you're trying to assess which way your commercial work leans on the scales of justice, you should aim to trade not on a celebrity's image, but on your own creative expression and commentary, in which celebrity images play a bit role. If Warhol could do it, so can you!

The core of trademark helps crafters too, protecting against consumer confusion in the search for quality products. But sometimes big trademark holders need to be reminded of their limits, particularly if your product is non-confusing, or is a parody that gets greater First Amendment leeway. As Judge Alex Kozinski, chief of the Ninth Circuit U.S. Court of Appeals, put it when ruling in *Mattel v. MCA Records* that the band Aqua didn't infringe Mattel's trademarks with their song "Barbie Girl": "The parties are advised to chill."

Wendy Seltzer is a fellow with Harvard's Berkman Center for Internet & Society and a visiting professor at Northeastern Law School. She leads the Chilling Effects Clearinghouse (chillingeffects.org).

Illustration by Damien Correll

Cute as a Button Bracelet

Spotlight a handful of your favorite buttons, vintage or new, with this easy project. Just thread them on wire to create a fun, instant-gratification bracelet!

You will need: Round- and flat-nose pliers, wire clippers, an assortment of buttons in the same color family (I used 11 pink buttons ranging from ⅜" to ¾" across), 18" of 24-gauge gold craft wire, clasp

1. Design.
Arrange your buttons in a row so that you like the mix of colors and sizes.

2. Thread.
Slip the wire through one of the holes of your first button, back to front, and hold the button about 6" from one end of the wire. Feed the working wire through the opposite hole, pulling it taut so that the button "sits" where you've placed it. Repeat with the next button, securing it close to the first one. Add more buttons until your string of wired buttons is about 6" long.

3. Trim.
Clip the wire ends so they're each 5"–6" long. Feed one of the ends back into the outermost hole of the last button, looping it through to reinforce it.

4. Loop.
Grasp the wire just above the button loop with your round-nose pliers, and make a neat 90° bend there (Figure A). Adjust the round-nose pliers so they're gripping to both sides of the wire bend, above and below it. Use flat-nose pliers to pull the wire tail over the end of the round-nose pliers and all the way around, creating a circle with a tail of wire still extending beyond it (Figure B).

5. Clasp.
Slip the clasp onto the loop (Figure C) and use flat-nose pliers to hold the circle while gripping the end of the wire tail with round-nose pliers. Slowly wrap the wire tail around, working from top to bottom, creating a neat coil (Figure D). Clip the end of the wire flush with the coil (Figure E), making sure the sharp tip isn't sticking out — if it is, use flat-nose pliers to flatten and smooth it into the coil. Repeat on the other side to add the other half of the clasp.

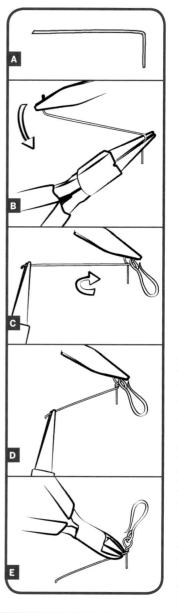

Susan Beal is a writer and crafter in Portland, Ore. This project is excerpted from her new jewelry-making book, *Bead Simple*, from Taunton Press. You can find more of her craft projects at susanbeal.com.

Photograph by Burcu Avsar and Zach DeSart; illustrations by Alexis Hartman

Craft: SPECIAL SECTION

SHOEWARE

Ah, shoes. Sure, they protect our feet, but let's face it: they also make a statement about who we are. In these pages, we have seven ways to customize your footgear that will show the world just how you roll.

Photograph by Garry McLeod

SHOE TIME

History shows it's human nature: we gotta have shoes. BY ARWEN O'REILLY

 15000 B.C.

The first documented shoes appear in pre-historic Spanish cave paintings showing animal skins wrapped around feet. »

8000 B.C.

Native Americans in Missouri leave behind the earliest surviving shoes.

4000 B.C.

In ancient Egypt, commoners wear sandals of woven papyrus or palm leaves. Pointed toes are reserved for royalty. ⌄

200 B.C.

Roman tragic actors wear platform shoes, sandals called *kothorni* with high wood or cork soles.

 mid-1500s

Venetian courtesans wear exquisitely decorated silk chopines up to 30" high (and have servants to help them walk). »

1605

A new last is developed which allows a sturdy, "true" heel to be worn in Queen Elizabeth's court (rumors of such things existing in Russia for centuries may have spurred this innovation). Men wear them as well as women for almost two centuries.

1628

Thomas Beard, a *Mayflower* pilgrim, nails together the first pair of Euro-shoes in America. Moccasins, which the natives have worn for centuries, become so popular that the colonies begin exporting them to England in 1650. »

1760

The first American factory for mechanized shoe production is established in Lynn, Mass.

 1940s

The cork platform and wedge make a comeback after centuries on the back burner. A shortage of leather in wartime leaves the cork soles exposed.

1951

The stiletto appears on the market, becoming standard wear by 1955. ⌄

1964

André Courrèges debuts a white plastic boot that is later named the go-go boot and enshrined in Nancy Sinatra's hit "These Boots Are Made for Walking." »

1972

Nike athletic shoes are launched by Oregon's Blue Ribbon Sports. The company is renamed Nike in 1978; the Nike Air debuts in 1979.

Illustrations by Tim Lillis

As anyone who's ever run out to get the paper in bare feet on a cold morning knows, shoes are a brilliant (and necessary) invention. People have been fascinated by footwear since the beginning of recorded history. The Greek god Mercury wore winged sandals (who doesn't want a pair of those?) and childhood fairy tales involving shoes abound: Cinderella, Puss in Boots, the Seven League Boots, the Little Old Woman Who Lived in a Shoe, not to mention Dorothy and her ruby slippers. Here's a brief timeline of shoe highlights throughout history.

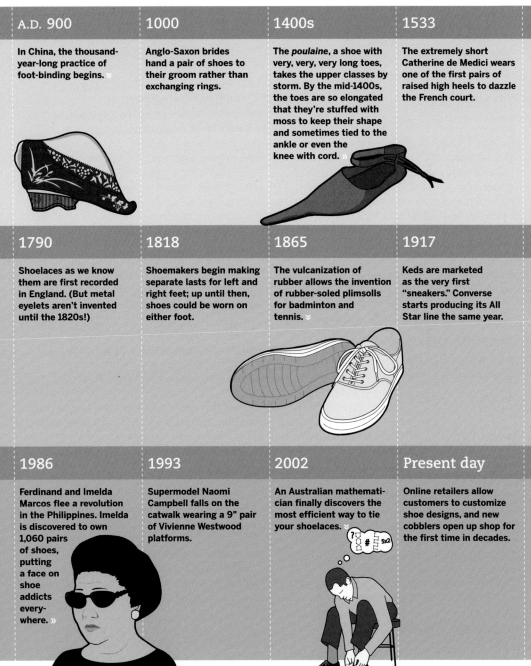

A.D. 900

In China, the thousand-year-long practice of foot-binding begins. »

1000

Anglo-Saxon brides hand a pair of shoes to their groom rather than exchanging rings.

1400s

The *poulaine*, a shoe with very, very, very long toes, takes the upper classes by storm. By the mid-1400s, the toes are so elongated that they're stuffed with moss to keep their shape and sometimes tied to the ankle or even the knee with cord. »

1533

The extremely short Catherine de Medici wears one of the first pairs of raised high heels to dazzle the French court.

1790

Shoelaces as we know them are first recorded in England. (But metal eyelets aren't invented until the 1820s!)

1818

Shoemakers begin making separate lasts for left and right feet; up until then, shoes could be worn on either foot.

1865

The vulcanization of rubber allows the invention of rubber-soled plimsolls for badminton and tennis. »

1917

Keds are marketed as the very first "sneakers." Converse starts producing its All Star line the same year.

1986

Ferdinand and Imelda Marcos flee a revolution in the Philippines. Imelda is discovered to own 1,060 pairs of shoes, putting a face on shoe addicts everywhere. »

1993

Supermodel Naomi Campbell falls on the catwalk wearing a 9" pair of Vivienne Westwood platforms.

2002

An Australian mathematician finally discovers the most efficient way to tie your shoelaces.

Present day

Online retailers allow customers to customize shoe designs, and new cobblers open up shop for the first time in decades.

DESIGN-AS-YOU-WEAR SANDALS

With Annie Mohaupt's wood-and-ribbon shoes, the wearer becomes the designer.

BY AMY O'NEILL HOUCK

If you've got the craft bug, and a house remodel means your basement is filled with power tools, where does that lead you? If you're Annie Mohaupt, it means reinventing the wheel, or rather, the shoe. Mohaupt's not unusual in loving shoes, but as a trained architect, she's constantly thinking about materials and how things are made. Often her musings stray from buildings to everyday objects. "When I walk around, I see materials and think, 'That would be great for a shoe.'"

As an architect, Mohaupt worked at a small firm in Chicago. She says her job, more project management than design, kept her behind a desk and away from the more artistic aspects of the profession she loved. "I wanted to do more with my hands." She made jewelry and handbags as a creative outlet.

> "I was inspired by a skateboard I saw, and it got me thinking about wooden shoes."

In 2005, a friend asked her to share a table at Chicago's Renegade Craft Fair. Mohaupt saw the fair as a new opportunity, and was excited to participate. "I wanted to create something other people weren't making."

It wasn't long before she came up with an idea: "I was inspired by a skateboard I saw, and it got me thinking about wooden shoes." Mohaupt devoted a summer to devising a new shoe design. She researched how skateboards were made, and how wood is bent for furniture. "I studied shoes that I thought were comfortable."

Mohaupt told herself, "If the shoes sell, I'll quit architecture." Even though it rained both days of the fair and attendance was low, she did well, and was convinced. She quit her job and founded Mohop Shoes.

The result of her research is a shoe that defies convention in many ways. The look has an air of Danish Modern furniture with clean lines and clear-finished wood. Wedges and heels come in three heights, and there are three toe shapes in the current collection — pointy, rounded, and an asymmetrical box shape. The shoes are made from solid cherry, walnut, or veneered birch plywood that Mohaupt imports from Finland, and some designs have abstract silk-screening on the wood base.

Though Mohaupt has refined her shoemaking process, she still makes each pair by hand. She's careful to use sustainable materials throughout her manufacturing process. She has incorporated recycled rubber soles and environmentally friendly glues and finishes. She screen-prints on the shoes, by hand, at Chicago's Screwball Press.

Mohaupt's shoes have caught the attention of fashionistas, greenies, and crafters because of the unusual materials and patent-pending design that features elastic loops secured to the base of the shoe with brass rivets. Each pair comes with a set of ribbons that can be laced through the loops and tied in various ways. The wearer becomes the shoe designer, choosing which ties to use and how to tie them. Wearers often come up with unusual ties of their own, incorporating buckles, vintage rickrack, or crocheted lace. As Mohaupt says on her website, "You can play Imelda Marcos without requiring the budget and storage space for 5,000 shoes."

➕ Annie Mohaupt's Mohop Shoes: mohop.com

Now turn the page for a DIY shoe-making lesson from Annie Mohaupt. »

Amy O'Neill Houck crochets, knits, and writes at her home in Washington, D.C. She blogs at hookandi.blogspot.com.

Photography by Brian Ulrich

SLIP-ON STYLE

Fashion new sandals that always match your whim. BY ANNIE MOHAUPT

Nearly as long as humankind has roamed the earth, people have been wearing shoes. Ancient Egyptians, Indians, and East Asians began sporting wooden sandals thousands of years ago. Thankfully, inexpensive power tools have sped up the tedious process of carving ergonomic shoes from slabs of wood. Add a few interchangeable ribbon ties, and you've got a modern twist to the ancient thong-style sandal. With a variety of wood finishes, footbed shapes, and ribbon styles, along with myriad ways to lace and tie the shoes, the design options for these sandals are nearly limitless. So take a cue from history and fashion yourself a custom pair of wooden kicks.

Read about Annie Mohaupt in the previous article, pages 42–43.

Photography by Annie Mohaupt

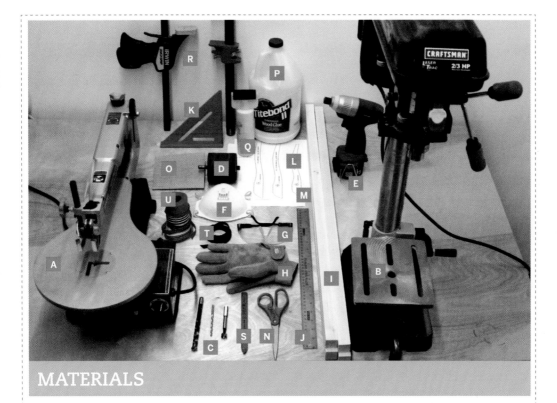

MATERIALS

» **[A] Scroll saw or band saw**

» **[B] Drill press**

» **[C] Drill bits:** ⅜" standard or Forstner, ⅛" standard, ½" Forstner

» **[D] Drum sander attachment,** 2" or 3", 120 or 150 grit

» **[E] Hand-held power drill**

» **[F] Dust mask**

» **[G] Eye protection**

» **[H] Work gloves**

» **[I] 1"×1"×36" square hardwood dowels (4)** or the equivalent of 10 linear feet

» **[J] Ruler**

» **[K] Square**

» **[L] Profile template** from craftzine.com/07/mohop

» **[M] Cardstock** or other heavy paper

» **[N] Scissors**

» **[O] Sandpaper** fine grit

» **[P] Wood glue** exterior grade

» **[Q] Glue roller** or foam paintbrush

» **[R] Clamps (6)** with at least a 6" opening

» **[S] Pen, pencil, and/or marker**

» **[T] ⅜" black grosgrain ribbon, about 18"**

» **[U] Other ribbons, fabric strips, elastic pieces, webbing, buckles of your choice**

» **Stain, paint, and/or sealer** (not shown)

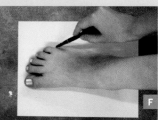

Fig. A: Use a square to draw lines perpendicular to the length of the wood. Fig. B: Align the heel of the profile template with the back edge of the wood. Fig. C: Cut just to the outside of the line.

Fig. D: Spread glue on the entire side profile. Fig. E: Clamp the stack of glued-together dowels and let them dry overnight. Fig. F: Trace your right foot onto a piece of cardstock.

⚠ CAUTION: Wear work gloves, a dust mask, and eye protection when using power tools!

1. Cut the dowels.

1a. Make a mark every 12" along the length of each dowel by using a square to draw lines perpendicular to the length of the wood (Figure A). Using the saw, cut the dowels along the lines, so you'll end up with at least ten 12"-long dowels. Each shoe uses 5 dowels.

NOTE: If you're using a band saw, you can start with two 1"×5"×12" pieces, rather than the dowels. Cut the profile once for each shoe, and skip the gluing steps.

1b. Print out the profile template from craftzine. com/07/mohop on cardstock. Cut out the template that matches your regular shoe size. Then align the heel of the profile template with the back edge of the wood (Figure B). Trace the profile on all 10 dowels.

1c. Using the saw, cut each of the dowels along the pattern line, taking care to cut as accurately as possible. It's better to cut just to the outside of the line (Figure C).

1d. Sand the cut edges lightly. You're just trying to remove splinters now, without reshaping the wood.

2. Glue the dowels.

2a. Spread a thin, even layer of glue on the entire side profile of a dowel using a glue roller or foam paintbrush (Figure D). Wipe off any excess glue. Set the dowel down with the gluey side up.

2b. Apply glue in the same manner to the opposite profile of another dowel. Stack the gluey side of this dowel onto the gluey side of the first dowel. Repeat these steps until you've glued a stack of 5 dowels.

2c. Clamp the stack of dowels together as tightly as you can, placing 1 clamp near the heel, 1 near the toe, and 1 at the mid-foot (Figure E). This may be tricky, as the glue makes the wood pieces slide around. Make sure all the dowels are aligned using the square. I just clamp the stack right to my tabletop.

2d. Repeat Steps 2a–2c, gluing and clamping the second set of 5 dowels. Let them dry overnight.

3. Design your footbed.

3a. Trace your right foot onto a piece of cardstock (Figure F).

3b. Using your foot shape as a guide, draw a plan

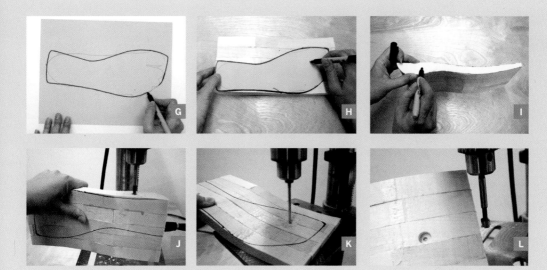

Fig. G: Draw a plan view for your shoe over your foot tracing. Fig. H: Place the template on the topside of one of the glued-up stacks. Fig. I: Mark the hole on your profile template according to your shoe size.

Fig. J: Drill a hole into the side of your shoe. Fig. K: Drill the thong hole perpendicularly through the top of the shoe. Fig. L: Drill a hole with the Forstner bit partway into the bottom of the shoe.

view for your shoe over the tracing (Figure G). Smooth out little bumps and create a nice toe and heel shape. You can make any shape you'd like — experiment with round, pointed, and square toes.

3c. This is now your plan template. Cut it out and place your foot on it again. Stick your pencil in the crotch between your big toe and second toe, and draw a little mark. This is the thong hole location. Using a sharp pencil, poke a hole in the template there.

3d. Unclamp your glued dowel stacks. Place the template on the topside of one of the glued-up stacks, aligning the back of the heel with the back of the dowels, and the right side of the template with the right side of the dowels (Figure H). Trace the plan onto the dowels, and mark the location of the thong hole.

3e. Turn your template over, and repeat the previous step on the other glue-up, mirroring the alignments with the back and left side of the left shoe.

4. Drill the holes.

4a. Using a sharp pencil, poke a hole in the center

of the "hole location" on your profile template according to your shoe size. Mark this hole location on the left side of the left shoe, and the right side of the right shoe (Figure I).

4b. Install the ⅜" bit in the drill press. Placing a shoe on its side, with the hole location facing up, drill a hole (Figure J). Your drill press may only be able to drill a couple of inches deep, which is fine. Drill as far as you can. Repeat with the other shoe.

4c. If the drill press doesn't drill all the way through, place the ⅜" bit into a hand drill, and drill the hole farther in. The hole you drilled earlier will keep you going in the correct direction. You may still not be able to drill all the way through the 5" dowel stack. That's fine, too — 3½" deep should be plenty to go all the way through the heel when the shoe is cut out.

4d. Install the ⅛" bit into the drill press. Hold the shoe firmly so the thong hole location will be drilled perpendicularly through the top of the shoe (the shoe will be rocked forward toward the toe, as shown in Figure K). Drill all the way through the shoe. Repeat with the other shoe.

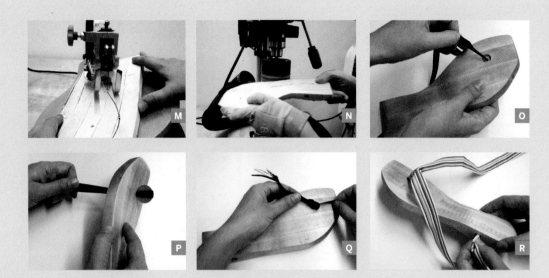

Fig. M: Carefully cut out the shoes along your plan line.
Fig. N: Sand each shoe until it's smooth to the touch.
Fig. O: Thread the narrow end of the ribbon through
the thong hole, from bottom to top.

Fig. P: Use a quarter to keep the loop 1" wide on the top
of the shoe. Fig. Q: Tie sturdy knots in the ribbon, then
trim the ends and dab them with glue. Fig. R: Lace a
ribbon through the thong loop and the hole in the back
of the shoe.

4e. Install the ½" Forstner bit in the drill press. Turn the shoes over and drill about ³⁄₁₆" to ¼" deep into the bottom of the shoe at the thong hole location using the existing ⅛" hole to center the hole you'll drill with the Forstner bit (Figure L, previous page).

5. Finish the shoes.

5a. Adjust the table on your saw to 20°. Carefully cut out the shoes along your plan line, making sure that the shoe is downhill from the saw blade (Figure M). This creates an elegant taper to the edge of the sandal.

5b. Install the sanding drum to the drill press. Sand each shoe until it's smooth to the touch, being careful not to sand so much that you change the size and shape of the shoes (Figure N).

TIP: I like to rig up a shop vac to collect sawdust from the drum, otherwise dust flies everywhere!

5c. Make the shoes extra-smooth with a quick sanding using fine-grit sandpaper. Then stain, paint, and/or seal the shoes according to the manufacturer's instructions. Set them out to dry.

5d. Cut the ³⁄₈" black grosgrain ribbon into two 9" lengths. With sharp scissors, trim the last inch on 1 end of each ribbon to about ⅛" wide.

5e. Thread the narrow end of the ribbon through the thong hole, from bottom to top (Figure O). At the top, leave a big loop in the ribbon. Taking care not to twist the ribbon, thread it back down.

5f. Pulling the ribbon from the bottom of the shoe, reduce the loop on the top to about 1" — to hold this size, it might help to stick a quarter in the loop (Figure P). Tie a sturdy knot or two on the ribbon (Figure Q), trim the ends, and dab a little glue on the knot, which should fit in the hole you made with the Forstner bit. Repeat with the other sandal.

5g. Lace a ribbon through the thong loop and the hole in the back of the shoe (Figure R), and tie however you want. Swap ribbons as often as you like. If lacing around your ankle, use stretchy ribbons for extra comfort.

NOTE: The shoes may be loud on hard surfaces. If you're shy with this kind of attention, visit your local cobbler and ask for soling that either you or he can attach.

BUSINESS REPLY MAIL
FIRST-CLASS MAIL   PERMIT NO 865   NORTH HOLLYWOOD CA

POSTAGE WILL BE PAID BY ADDRESSEE

NO POSTAGE
NECESSARY
IF MAILED
IN THE
UNITED STATES

Craft:

PO BOX 17046
NORTH HOLLYWOOD CA 91615-9588

CONVERSE À LA MOD

When it comes to shoe projects, Converse All Stars is a brand we love to mod. Originally created in 1917 as basketball shoes, "Chucks" (nicknamed after hoops star Chuck Taylor) quickly became one of the most popular shoe brands of all time. It's their playful shape, easy-to-cut canvas, accessibility, and relative low cost that make these sneakers the most fun to hack. So try the following fabric swap and knitted Chuck projects and consider yourself a Converse crafter.

THE ALL STAR FABRIC SWAP

Restyle your classic Chucks with simple sewing and shoe glue.
BY TOM WYATT

I bought my first pair of All Stars about a year ago and wore them almost constantly, until they finally fell apart. In the end it was only my girlfriend's nagging (and eventually her putting them in the bin) that tore them away from me.

All my Converse sneakers eventually fall apart in the same way — the fabric in the back rips away from the sole, but the rubber itself is fine. Shortly after realizing this, I rescued a pair from the rubbish and started pulling them apart, trying to work out how I could create a pattern for them with new fabric. Here's what I came up with.

Tom Wyatt is a 26-year-old IT engineer who enjoys pulling things apart and occasionally putting them back together again. He recently branched out to fabric.

MATERIALS

- » **Used pair of Converse All Stars shoes**

- » **Cotton fabric of your choice** I used quilting fabric, which isn't particularly thick or hard-wearing. It's probably best to back it with canvas, like the originals are made of.

- » **Scissors and craft knife**

- » **Sewing machine**

- » **Eyelet punch kit** such as the Crop-A-Dile Eyelet and Snap Punch kit, which you can find online for about $25.

- » **Shoe Goo shoe glue**

1. Cut the fabric off the shoe.

Take a craft knife and cut the old fabric uppers off the sole, removing the insole as well (Figure A, next page). Do this carefully so that you don't hurt any part of the rubber shoe.

Try and remove the fabric in one piece, as we need it for the next step. Also, carefully cut out the "Converse All Star" circle label and save it for later.

NOTE: You may want to start with only one shoe, saving the other as a reference for the placement of the border stitch, Converse label, and shoelace holes.

2. Make the pattern.

You should have the 1 large piece of fabric you've just removed from the shoe, plus the tongue (Figure B). Cut the large piece in half down the back of the shoe. Place the 2 halves on a large sheet of paper

and trace around them (Figure C). When tracing their bottom edges, trace 1" away from the fabric so that you'll have extra fabric to tuck under the insole later. Trace the tongue, adding 1" extra at the toe end.

3. Cut out the pattern.

Cut out the paper pattern you just made. Fold the new fabric in half so that it's doubled up, and pin the paper templates to it as shown in Figure D.

4. Cut out the fabric.

With your pattern pinned to the fabric, cut around the pattern, making sure to cut approximately ¼" outside the lines (Figure D).

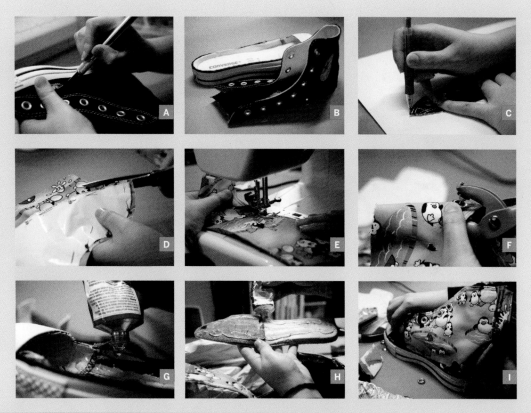

5. Sew it all up.

Face the right sides of the fabric uppers together (wrong sides facing out) and sew together the side where the back of the shoe will be. Then turn them right-side out and iron them flat.

Using the other shoe for reference, sew the standard decorative Converse border stitches around the panel and down the back (Figure E). Then glue the "Converse All Star" label back onto the shoe. Once it's firmly in place, hand-sew along the edge of the label to further secure it.

6. Punch holes for the laces.

With an eyelet punch, set seven or eight 4mm eyelets along one edge of the panel, for the laces. Repeat on the other side (Figure F).

NOTE: Read the instructions for Shoe Goo or any other type of glue you use before applying it to this project.

7. Glue your fabric to the sole.

Smear Shoe Goo around the inside edges of the sole and inside the toe cap (Figure G).

Stick the tongue in and shove a wad of paper in there to apply pressure to it.

Stick the edges of the fabric uppers to the top of the sole and inside the toe, then pack the inside of the shoe with paper to apply pressure while the glue is drying. Insert the insole and apply more glue around the edges to fix the uppers to the insole (Figures H and I). Allow at least 24 hours of drying time before wearing the shoes.

My shoes have held up nicely, and when they do wear out, I'll just make myself another pair!

HOTSHOT HIGH-TOPS

Deconstruct and reconstruct your old standbys with new knitting.

BY KATIE TESAROWSKI

A friend once teased me about my addiction to knitting. He pointed out that I had knit practically an entire wardrobe for myself: sweaters, skirts, hats, gloves, scarves, bikinis, socks, and slippers. The one item he said I was missing was a pair of shoes. Rather than get offended, I took that as a personal challenge.

Though I wasn't brave enough to knit a pair of shoes from scratch, I dug through my closet for a pair of old shoes I could modify, and found a ratty pair of Converse sneaks. I copied the shape of the high-tops, and ended up with a shoe strong enough to wear while playing a game of baseball! The following pattern is for a Converse shoe size 8.

Katie Tesarowski enjoys developing her own knitting patterns and working creatively with yarn. She's currently studying the tuba at the University of Lethbridge in Alberta, Canada.

Photography by Garry McLeod

MATERIALS

- » Pair of high-top Converse sneakers

- » 2 skeins Red Heart Super Saver acrylic yarn I used 1 Forest Green, 1 White.

- » Spool of heavy-duty thread

- » Sewing needle

- » Tapestry/yarn needle

- » Scissors

- » Thimble

- » Gauge: 2" = 7 stitches, 9 rows
  Needles: U.S. size 6

Abbreviations:
K = Knit
P = Purl
YO = Yarn over
K2tog = Knit 2 together
M1 = Increase by 1 stitch, also known as KFB
(knit in the front and back of the stitch)

1. Prepare the shoes.

Except for the strip of fabric that runs along the heel of the shoe, which provides stability to the framework, cut away the fabric uppers, leaving only ¼" still attached to the soles.

2. Knit.

Each shoe is made from 3 separate pieces of knitting: 2 pieces that form the sides of the shoe and 1 tongue.

Piece A: Left Side (2)
Cast on 28 stitches.
Row:
1) K
2) P
3) K12, YO, K2tog, K1, YO, K2tog, K (28 sts)
4) P2tog, P (27 sts)
5) K23, YO, K2tog, K2tog (26 sts)
6) P
7) K20, YO, K2tog, K2, K2tog (25 sts)
8) P
9) K17, YO, K2tog, K2, cast off 4. This should be the end of the row; leave enough of a tail to weave it in later. Rejoin at the other end of the piece and purl row 10, staying in stocking stitch.
10) P
11) K15, YO, K2tog, cast off 4 (17 sts). Repeat the same process as row 9.
12) P
13) K
14) P

15) K13, YO, K2tog, K2 (17 sts)
16) P2tog, P
17) K14, K2tog (15 sts)
18) P
19) K11, YO, K2tog, K2
20) P2tog, P (14 sts)
21) K
22) P
23) Cast off all stitches.

Piece B: Right Side (2)
This makes the mirror image of Piece A.
Row:
1) K
2) P
3) K
4) P to last 2 stitches, P2tog (27 sts)
5) K2tog, K2tog, YO, K (26 sts)
6) P
7) K2tog, K2, K2tog, YO, K (25 sts)
8) P
9) Cast off 4, K2, K2tog, YO, K (21 sts)
10) P
11) Cast off 4, K2tog, YO, K (17 sts)
12) P
13) K
14) P
15) K2, K2tog, YO, K (17 sts)
16) P to last 2 stitches, P2tog (16 sts)
17) K2tog, K (15 sts)
18) P
19) K2, K2tog, YO, K (15 sts)

20) P to last 2 stitches, P2tog (14 sts)
21) K
22) P
23) Cast off all stitches.

Piece C: Shoe Tongue (2)
Cast on 9 stitches.
K 5 rows in garter stitch.
Row 6: K1, M1, K3, M1, K1 (11 sts).
K 25 more rows in garter stitch.
Cast off all stitches.

3. Add knitting pieces.
With the tapestry needle, weave in all yarn ends.
Thread a sewing needle, with the thread doubled for
extra strength. Begin to sew each piece to its spot
on the shoe.

Start with the heel, and sew forward to the toe.
You'll need to stretch the knitting slightly to make it
fit the entire length of the shoe so it won't be baggy.

It's helpful to use a thimble, since the canvas on
the shoes is reinforced in the heel and toe with
plastic, and it's harder to push the needle through
in those places.

4. Sew on the logos.
Cut the circular Converse logos off the shoe fabric you removed. Using the sewing needle, punch
holes around the edges of the patches. This makes
it much easier to sew them onto your new shoes.
Thread the needle, and sew the patches onto the
ankles of the shoes, going through the holes you've
already punched.

5. Lace 'em!
Remove the shoelaces from the canvas shoes, and
lace them into the eyelets made from yarn-overs.
Try them on, and take them for a run!

BABY STEPS

Make soft, pliable shoes for your favorite toddler. BY EVE OKI SHIRLEY

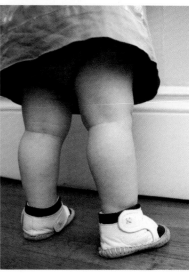

A good pair of shoes gives us the opportunity to strike the fine balance between great design and function — and that goes for baby shoes, too. Babies' feet are soft and flexible, so they can be squeezed into almost any shoe. But because their bone structure is still taking shape, it's not a good idea to force their spongy little piggies into hard-shelled receptacles.

The shoes I've designed here, for babies between the ages of 6 and 14 months, have just the right amount of structure to support the feet, but still allow them a wide range of motion. The leather supports comfortably and breathes naturally. And the velcro flaps and big openings make getting them on and off fuss-free.

Eve Oki Shirley is a shoemaker. Having just moved from Tokyo to Las Vegas, she looks forward to opening her custom-made shoe store sometime in the near future. For her latest creations, check out www.eviok.com.

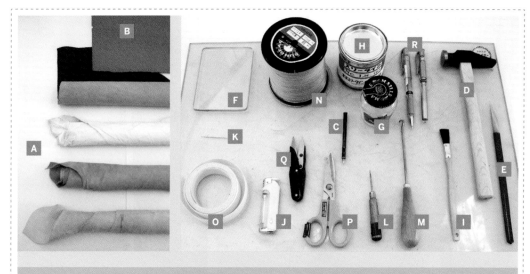

MATERIALS

» **[A] Leather** The optimal thickness/weight for each piece:

    Sole and insole: ³⁄₃₂"–¹⁄₈" (3oz–3½oz)
    Uppers: ¹⁄₁₆"–³⁄₁₆" (1oz–3oz)
    Toe piece and lining: no more than ¹⁄₁₆" (1oz)
    Ankle piece: ¹⁄₁₆"–³⁄₁₆" (1oz–3oz)
      but you must be able to skive, or scrape, thin slices off

» **[B] Sponge** ¹⁄₈"–³⁄₁₆" thick for cushioning around heels

» **[C] Hole punch** such as the Mini Leather Punch (michaels.com) or the ¹⁄₁₆" Craftool Drive Punch (tandyleatherfactory.com)

» **[D] Hammer** ideally with a round face to avoid damaging the leather

» **[E] X-Acto knife** Use a new, sharp blade.

» **[F] Glass surface** or marble slab for skiving

» **[G] Soft glue such as rubber cement** for a temporary hold

» **[H] Hard glue such as contact cement** for a permanent hold

» **[I] Brush for the glue** A thinning agent helps to keep the brush clean.

» **[J] Lighter**

» **[K] Round-tip needle** for cross-stitching

» **[L] Pick or scratch awl**

» **[M] Hook tool**

» **[N] Waxed nylon thread** or artificial sinew

» **[O] Velcro, 1¼" wide** The adhesive-backed kind is easy to use.

» **[P] Regular scissors**

» **[Q] Small embroidery scissors** or nipper

» **[R] Silver and/or gold pen** Try the Uni-ball Gel Impact, which cleans off easily. Use silver for darker leather and gold for lighter leather.

[NOT SHOWN]

» **Sewing machine**

» **Cutting board**

Folding line

Skive the very
edge at a 45°
angle.

Then skive wider

A

B

Fig. A: The pieces you'll need are: (left to right)
green = soles, pink = sponge, white = uppers 1 and 2,
brown = toe and ankle pieces, white = lining.

Fig. B: The top illustration is your folding line. First
skive the very edge to determine how far you want to
skive, then add width. Make sure to go a little over the
folding line.

1. Prepare the pattern.
Print out 2 copies of the pattern from craftzine.com/
07/babyshoes. Use one as a guide (set aside for later)
and the other as an actual pattern. Using the punch
and hammer, punch out all the dots on the pattern.

2. Cut the leather and sponge.
2a. Place the pattern pieces on the appropriate
thicknesses of leather. Trace all outlines and holes
using the silver or gold pen. Make sure to mark the
center and inside edge (|| = inside edge) of each
piece because it can be hard to distinguish left from
right once the pieces are all cut out.

**NOTE: The patterns are created just for the left side of
each piece. Flip them and repeat the steps to complete
the right side.**

2b. Cut the traced pieces using your X-Acto knife.
For outlines, it's better to cut along the inside of the
line rather than on or outside the line.

2c. Cut the sponge in the same manner (Figure A).

3. Skive the leather.
Skiving means thinning leather in order to make
it easier to stitch. Since the machine that can do

this is prohibitively expensive, we'll skive by hand
using a knife (Figures B–F).

3a. Following Figure B, trace the inner line of the
pattern onto the leather anklepiece. Skive it on all
edges. The topside will need to be folded later, so
the end should be paper-thin. The bottom piece will
simply be glued and stitched, so you should skive to
about half of the starting thickness.

3b. There will be a total of 4 layers at the toe area
on the final product. Depending on the thickness
of your leather, it may become very difficult to stitch.
Skive the area with the crossed lines on the pattern
(uppers 1 and 2) down to about $2/3$ or $1/2$ of the
starting thickness.

4. Punch holes.
4a. Following the pattern, punch out all the red dots
(Figure G, next page).

4b. Apply hard glue on the back of the toe piece
and on upper 1 where the toe piece will be placed.

4c. Wait until the glue is completely dry on each
piece, then attach them.

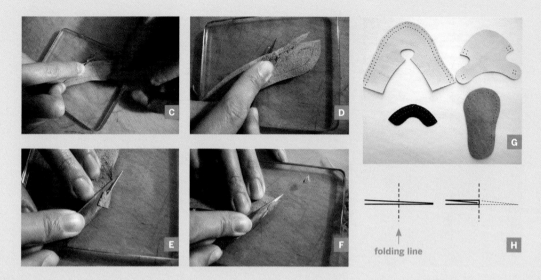

Fig. C: Skive the very edge. Fig. D: Then go wider.
Fig. E: For paper-thin skives, cut from inside to outside.
Fig. F: Repeat several times to achieve an even taper.

Fig. G: The pieces that require punching.
Fig. H: The folding diagram for the ankle piece.

folding line

4d. Punch out the holes on the toe piece marked by the blue dots (Figure I).

5. Fold the leather.

5a. Trace the erased inner line again on the back and the front of the ankle piece (Figure J).

5b. Using the knife, make tiny slits, more or less evenly spaced around the top edge, but closer together around the corners (Figure K).

5c. Lightly apply the soft glue, wait until it dries, then start folding the flaps along the inner line using an awl. The soft glue is forgiving, so you can easily detach and try again (Figure L).

5d. Hammer down the edge to make it flat (Figure M).

5e. For the sponge, apply the hard glue on all the edges. Wait until it's dry, then poke down the middle with the awl and squeeze both ends together to make a tapered edge (Figure N).

6. Add an accent.

6a. Using the same waxed thread as you will for the final stitching, stitch a cross at each flap on upper 1.

Go through twice, just to add a little volume, if you choose. Or you can sew on a small button or other customized design. Have fun with it! If you choose the cross, make a tight knot twice and cut the thread, leaving about ¼" on both ends (Figure O1, page 60).

6b. Using the lighter, burn the ends of the thread. The wax and the nylon thread will start to melt. Quickly blow out the flame and hammer down the end to squish it and make one glob (Figure O2). You'll do the same thing for the final stitching as well.

7. Attach the velcro.

7a. For each shoe, cut 2 lengths of velcro tape 1⅜" long, with the hook sides and loop sides still fastened together. Peel off the adhesive backing (or apply soft glue if the velcro doesn't have adhesive) on the loop (soft) sides and attach them to the 2 flaps on upper 1 (Figure P).

7b. Shape the tape with scissors, then pull off the hook (hard) sides and attach them to upper 2, where it's marked (Figure Q).

7c. On the reverse side of the leather, lightly mark where you'll stitch the velcro with a semi-sharp tool

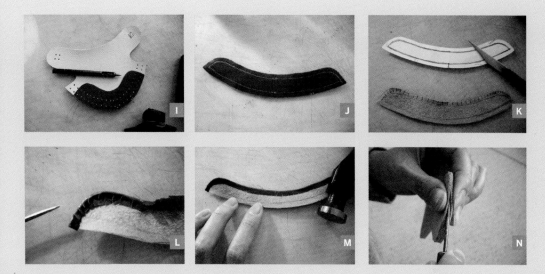

Fig. I: Punch holes in toe piece only after gluing.
Fig. J: Trace inner line on ankle piece. Fig. K: Make tiny
slits on the upper edge. Fig. L: Carefully fold flaps,
using the awl.

Fig. M: Hammer them down to flatten.
Fig. N: Taper sponge edges like so.

like the back of a knife or scissors. Then sew all 4
velcro pieces onto the leather (Figures R–S).

7d. After each sewing, pull the front thread through
to the back side and tie two knots. Carefully burn the
knot with the lighter to make a very tiny melted knot.

8. Sew the pieces together.

8a. Start with the heels. Turn upper 2 inside out,
and sew the heel at the very edge (Figure T). Be
careful not to sew over the holes at the end!

8b. Turn upper 2 right-side out and hammer along
the stitched line to flatten the edge.

8c. To sew the ankle piece, flip over upper 2 and
lightly apply hard glue to the top inside edge.
Also lightly apply hard glue to the bottom outside
edge of the ankle piece. Wait until completely dry,
then attach the 2 pieces, starting from the center
(should be marked with a silver dot) and working
out to the sides. Sew along the edge (Figure U).

8d. Sew the lining and the toe piece. Flip upper 2
inside out. Lightly apply soft glue on the back side
of upper 2 and the lining. Wait until it's dry, then
put the 2 pieces together, starting from the center
and working out to the sides (Figure V). Flip them
back again, right-side out, and sew along the edge,
starting from the beginning of the ankle piece to
the end. Sew the toe piece along the edge.

**NOTE: I put these 2 steps together to minimize changing
the thread on your sewing machine. These are the last
stitches that require brown thread for the top and white
for the bottom.**

9. Attach the sponge.

9a. Detach the lining and upper where they were
just glued, and reapply soft glue on the back of the
upper and front of the sponge piece. Wait until it's
dry and carefully place the sponge, starting at the
top center and working out to the sides. It may be
difficult at first and the sponge may seem too short,
but it should fit right into both edges after a couple
of tries (Figure W).

You can also start this step by turning the piece
inside out, but turn it over immediately after attaching the sponge at the center. Because of the radius
of the flipped upper, the sponge will seem much too
short if placed inside out!

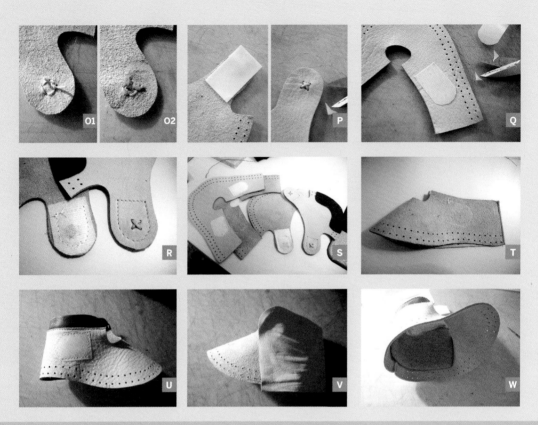

Fig. O: Finishing the accents. Fig. P: Attach velcro to flap first, then cut excess corners. Fig. Q: Detach the hook side, and glue on upper 2. Fig. R: Stitch velcro like so. Fig. S: The velcro patches all sewn on.

Fig. T: When sewing, start with the heel. Fig. U: Ankle piece sewn. Fig. V: Lining temporarily held with soft glue for sewing. Fig. W: Sponge is glued and placed like so.

9b. Glue the lining, making sure to glue the bottom near the holes (Figure X).

9c. Punch holes in the lining. Follow the holes on the upper, and simply re-punch where the existing holes are. Be careful not to punch over the sewn thread!

9d. Using the nipper, carefully cut out any excess lining from the top, and below the upper (Figure Y).

10. Stitch the shoe together.

The final pieces are: upper 1, upper 2, sole, and insole.

10a. Cut waxed thread (or artificial sinew) to 72". Using a blanket stitch, start at the top hole on the right side of the heel, inside to out. Leave about 5" of thread (so that you can pull it by hand later).

10b. Go from the bottom sole to bottom hole to upper hole, and wrap around the thread (refer to Figures Z and AA). Repeat the steps to hole 14. (See the pattern for hole numbers.)

10c. At hole 15 (which should be marked with a silver dot), begin stitching upper 1. Repeat the same steps, but simply place upper 1 in between the sole and upper 2.

10d. After adding upper 1, you may not be able to do the entire stitch in one go as shown in the diagram. Don't worry — just stitch 1 hole at a time. It might get a bit confusing, especially

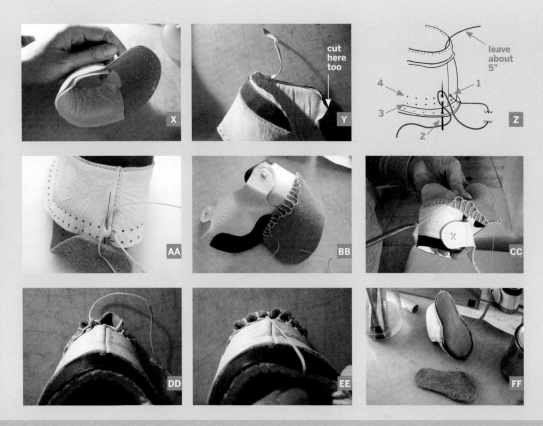

Fig. X: Make sure to glue the bottom together for re-punching! Fig. Y: Cut the excess lining. Figs. Z & AA: How to begin stitching. Fig. BB: It's OK if it doesn't look like a shoe yet. Fig. CC: Use the hook tool to tighten. Fig. DD: After stitching, the sole is usually uneven. Fig. EE: Pull with your needle to space the sole evenly. Fig. FF: Hard to turn the shoe inside out? It's much easier to glue the insole this way.

when the thread is long; just focus on the order of the stitch.

10e. Don't worry if the stitches are loose (Figure BB). Stitch to about halfway, then start tightening the thread with the hook tool (Figure CC). When tightened, the top part of the thread should sit right around the edge of the sole. After stitching all around, the sole may be uneven (Figure DD). If so, use the needle to make an even crease (Figure EE).

10f. Finish off your stitching where the first thread came out. Both threads should end inside the shoe. Pull both ends tightly as you flip the shoe inside out, just enough to expose the ends (you don't have to turn the shoe entirely).

10g. As you did with the accent on the flap, make 2 tight knots and cut off the thread, leaving about ¼" on each end. Carefully burn the ends using the lighter, and quickly blow the flame out before it reaches the knot. While still hot, hammer down the end to make one glob of knot.

11. Attach the insole.
There are 2 ways to glue the insole. You can glue the front half of the insole and the shoe, then do the back half.

Or you can slowly turn the entire shoe inside out and do it in one shot (Figure FF). Always wait until the glue on each piece is completely dry, then attach. Use hard glue for a permanent hold.

ROLL BABY ROLL!

Transform any shoes into hot roller skates and go on with your bad self!

BY LUANNE TEOH
& RICHARD HUMPHREY

So why would you want to make your own roller skates? Because you can! Imagine rolling into a rink and turning heads as skaters check out your original, cool-looking skates. Not only will your custom skates set you apart in terms of style, fit, and comfort, they're also a great conversation piece with the irresistible appeal of being able to say you made them yourself. The coolness factor is priceless!

A well-made pair of custom roller skates can last you years, with countless hours of fun to be had. Studies show that 1 hour of moderate roller-skating by a 140-pound person burns 330 calories, and vigorous skating burns up to 590 calories. Apart from the health benefits, skating is also a great way to socialize at the rink or park.

Follow this step-by-step guide carefully to ensure the safety of your skates. And of course, always remember to wear protective gear when skating!

■◖ See the how-to video at craftzine.com/07/skates

Luanne Teoh is the business developer for skates.com, retailers of roller skates and skateboards since 1975. Richard Humphrey has been a professional skater since 1978 and is the creator of rollerdance.com.

Photograph by Garry McLeod

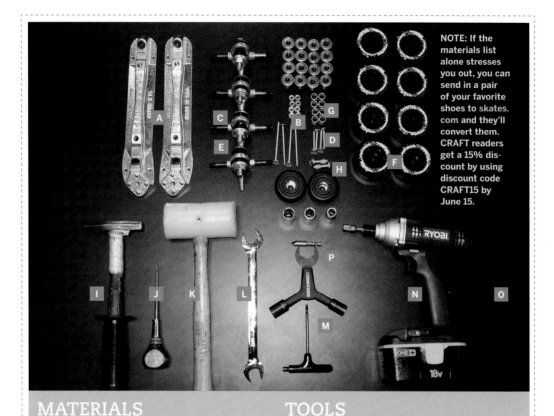

NOTE: If the materials list alone stresses you out, you can send in a pair of your favorite shoes to skates.com and they'll convert them. CRAFT readers get a 15% discount by using discount code CRAFT15 by June 15.

MATERIALS

» Cool, flat-soled shoes (not shown)

» [A] Aluminum roller skate plates (1 pair)

» [B] Mounting bolts and nuts (8)

» [C] Trucks (4)

» [D] Snyder cups (8) These back the head of the mounting bolt so it won't pull through the sole of the shoe.

» [E] Kingpins (4) These hold the trucks together and attach them to the plate.

» [F] Wheels (8) indoor or outdoor

» [G] Axle nuts (8)

» [H] 5/16" or 5/8" toe stop bolts (2) depending on the plate you choose

TOOLS

» [I] Small hammer

» [J] Hole punch or Sharpie marker

» [K] Rubber or plastic mallet

» [L] 9/16" and 11/16" flat open-end wrenches

» [M] Skate bearing press (optional) handy to install or remove wheel bearings

» [N] Drill and 3/8" bit

» [O] Stable 2"×4" wooden or metal platform to hold the shoe upside down

» [P] Skate tools flathead bit (or screwdriver), Power Dyne tool with 1/2" and 9/16" sockets and 15/16" wrench, and Snyder breaker bar (not shown) to break off mounting bolts

All parts are available from skates.com.

Fig A: Plate alignment. Figs. B–C: Marking the drill holes on the shoe soles. Fig. D: Precision drilling. Figs. E–F: The Snyder cup and mounting bolt installation.

Fig. G: Tapping the plate into place. Fig. H: Tightening the bolt nuts. Fig. I: Breaking off the bolt with a special Snyder break-off tool.

9 Steps to Roller Skates

1. Select the shoe. Pick one with a flat sole. The plate that will be attached to the shoe needs to have contact against the sole.

2. Select the plate size based on the size of your shoe. The plate should be centered on the sole and shouldn't stick over the front or back of the shoe. Line the plate up accurately before drilling.

3. Use a punch or a marker to mark the drill hole locations on the shoe soles, using the holes on the plate as a guide (Figures A–C). Four holes are required for each skate. Proceed to drill all the holes, not exceeding 1" depth on the front holes and 1"–2" depth in the heels (Figure D).

4. Once the holes are drilled, put the Snyder cups in place inside the shoe and insert the mounting bolts through them: 2 in the front and 2 in the rear (Figures E–F). Now place the plate onto the mounting bolts, using a soft mallet to tap it into place (Figure G). Repeat for the other shoe.

5. Secure the plates by tightening the mounting bolt nuts onto the mounting bolts, starting with the rear 2 nuts (Figure H). Using a special Snyder break-off tool, break off the long end of each mounting bolt so that it's flush with the mounting bolt nut (Figure I).

NOTE: At this point, use a small hammer to flatten the ends of the mounting bolts so there are no rough edges.

6. Mount all 4 trucks. Start by loosening up the

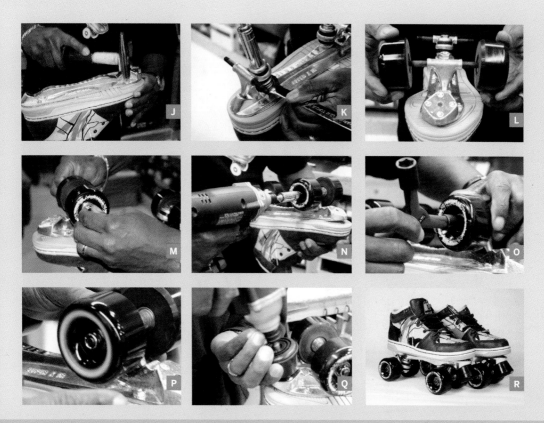

Figs. J–K: Installing, tightening, and adjusting the truck and kingpin. Figs L–O: Wheel placement and fine tuning. Fig. P: Fine tuning the axle nut. Fig. Q: Mounting the toe stop. Fig. R: The complete skate assembly, ready to roll.

kingpin nut about ¼ turn. Now hand-tighten the kingpin into the plate. This will eliminate any chance of stripping the threads inside the plate. Once the kingpin is in place, tighten the kingpin nut to the base of the plate. Using an ¹¹⁄₁₆" open wrench, back off the nut 1 turn. Then, using a ⁹⁄₁₆" socket wrench, tighten the kingpin into the plate, compressing the cushions slightly (Figure K).

NOTE: Do not overcompress the cushions. This will cause the skate to have no side-to-side movement.

This step is one of the most crucial parts of adjusting a skate for movement. If too loose, the skate will tend to lean too much to the left or right without any control. If too tight, the skate will act on its own by shifting more to one side than the other. With both hands on the truck, test the movement for insufficient or excess play in the trucks, and adjust accordingly.

7. Place the wheels on the axles and position each axle nut in place (Figures L–P). Using a drill or skate tool and a ½" socket, tighten each axle nut firmly onto the wheel. Once firm, back the axle nut off ⅛ of a turn to allow the wheels to spin freely. Test by spinning the wheel with your hand. If the wheel abruptly stops, slight adjustment is needed.

8. Install the toe stops, using a ⁵⁄₁₆" or ⅝" bolt depending on your plate (Figure Q).

9. Inspect the skates thoroughly. Lace up and roller-skate on a smooth surface. You're now ready to roll in your custom-made roller skates!

SHOE MODS MADE SIMPLE

Check out these easy ways to make your shoes all your own.
BY IVORY EILEEN

A doodle is a type of sketch, an unfocused drawing made while a person's attention is otherwise occupied. They are simple drawings that can have a meaning, a shape, or just irregular forms. —Wikipedia

The doodler in my house is my sweetheart, Mike T. He's always drawing on something. I ask him, "Can you put some color into my shoes, maybe match them to my skirt?" and in about 5 minutes I have a brand-new pair of shoes — custom! Here are two easy ways you can do it, too.

LEFT: Stencils and spray paint. RIGHT: Doodles!

Stencils and Spray Paint

MATERIALS
» **Newspaper**
» **Tape** Masking tape works well.
» **Stencils** These can be store-bought, such as drafting templates, or you can make your own by drawing designs on cardstock and cutting them out.
» **Spray paint** Any kind will work.

NOTE: You must be 18 or older to buy spray paint in the store. If you can't get spray paint, just use the Sharpie paint pens with your stencil.

1. Cover your work area with newspaper.

2. Tape off any part of the shoe where you don't want the paint to go. If there are buttons or straps that should stay the way they are, tape them up. You can also stuff the shoes with newspaper; this helps the surface stay firm and keeps the paint out.

3. Hold the stencil firmly against the surface of the shoe, shake the can of paint first, then give a little spray. (You can test the spray first on the newspaper before you really go for it!)

Wipe the wet paint off the stencil with some newspaper — always keep it dry! — and spray again.

4. You can layer stencils, for instance yellow moons and red stars, to make your shoes multicolored.

Doodle by Hand with Paint Pens

MATERIALS
» **Sharpie oil-based paint markers**
These come in 4 sizes and 15 colors.

1. Have fun, and doodle away!
Yes, that's all there is to it! Random lines, shapes, and patterns don't require a big plan or very much thought. Just think about the color scheme: what colors will work well together, and whether they'll go with your favorite handbag.

Ivory Eileen is an art docent and jewelry-maker living in Sonoma County, Calif. You can see her work at paperorganics.com.

Photograph by Sam Murphy, illustrations on shoes by Mike Thibault

Craft:
PROJECTS

With winter behind us, it's the perfect time for these warm-weather projects. Sew up a Japanese yukata (a lightweight jacket) and make these strappy shoes for some outdoor fun. Build a set of portable speakers and create a beautiful batik design on fabric. Now you have the accoutrements for a day in the park.

Photograph by Garry McLeod

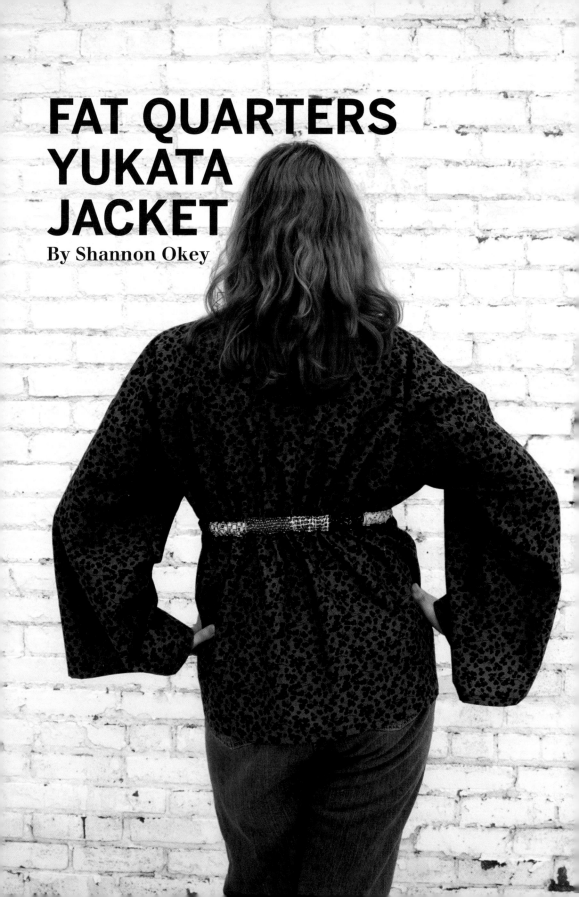

FAT QUARTERS YUKATA JACKET

By Shannon Okey

THIS JAPANESE-INSPIRED COTTON JACKET IS GREAT FOR SPRING AND SUMMER WEATHER.

▶ Although *yukata* (浴衣) literally means "bathing clothes" in Japanese, these straight-seamed, unlined cotton robes are not limited to after-bath time. An alternative to heavier silk kimonos, they also make perfect wraps when going out in warmer weather.

This jacket takes traditional yukata construction and turns it on its head, using an elasticized band at the center back to draw in the sides without using darts, and replacing the obi with a clever knotted cord and button closure.

More a recipe than an exact pattern, the design is easily adaptable to a variety of body shapes and sizes (hey, even sumo wrestlers sport yukatas!), and it lets you use up lots of those fat quarters and cotton scraps that are taking up space in your craft room.

» Professional Japanese sumo wrestlers must wear a traditional yukata robe with wooden sandals called *geta* when out in public during wrestling season.

» Marc Jacobs has his own line of modern yukata fashions featuring bold colors and whimsical patterns, available only in Japan.

» A fat quarter is a quarter-yard cut of fabric that measures 18"×22" and is shaped more like a square. A regular quarter yard is a 9"×44" strip, cut from selvedge to selvedge.

Photography by Shannon Okey; illustrations by Tim Lillis

Shannon Okey is the author of 10+ crafty books and can be found online at knitgrrl.com.

WHAT YOU'LL NEED

[A] Iron

[B] 1" heavy waistband elastic, 15" length

[C] ½yd contrasting cotton fabric or several fat quarters

[D] Ruler

[E] Cotton quilting fabric, **about 2yds** depending on width (see sizing in Step 1)

If your local fabric store doesn't have any fabric that strikes your fancy, check out reprodepot.com or purlsoho.com — and if you can't find something you like there, I don't know what to tell you!

[F] Scissors

[G] Coordinating thread

[H] Measuring tape

[I] Large button, 1½"

[J] Loop turner or safety pin

[K] Straight pins

[NOT SHOWN]

Sewing machine (optional) makes it go much faster!

Pattern available at craftzine.com/07/jacket

⏩ SEW AN ORIGINAL JACKET FROM YOUR FAVORITE FABRICS

Time: 2–3 Hours Complexity: Easy

BEFORE YOU START

If you're using new fabric or a variety of cottons that may shrink at different rates, put them through a hot wash and cold rinse in your washing machine to ensure they've shrunk as much as they can before you start to cut and sew. This is especially important if you plan to sew different fabrics together in patchwork or strips.

1. MEASURE

1a. Ask someone to measure you across your upper back, from one arm to the other, with the measuring tape. If you don't have a helper, find a sweater that fits you well and measure across the top — at shoulder level, not bust. In either case, add 2" and that's your measurement A.

1b. Measure the length of your arm, from the top of your shoulder to the wrist. Add 1" and that's measurement B.

1c. Holding your arms out from your body, measure from the top of your shoulder to the center of your bust. Multiply by 2 and add 1". This is measurement C, the width of your sleeve pieces.

1d. Measure across your chest at bust level. Each front panel is generally ⅓ the width of the back, but if you are large-chested, you may need to make your front panels wider to accommodate your bust. If this measurement is larger than A, take note, and it will be measurement D.

1e. Decide how long you want your jacket to be. Measure from the nape of your neck to just below your hip. Add 2", and this is measurement E.

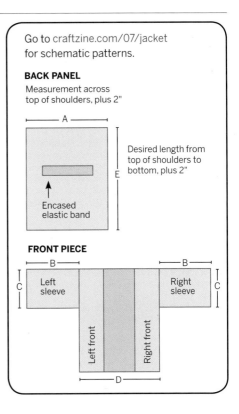

Go to craftzine.com/07/jacket for schematic patterns.

BACK PANEL
Measurement across top of shoulders, plus 2"

A

Desired length from top of shoulders to bottom, plus 2"

E

Encased elastic band

FRONT PIECE

B

B

C

Left sleeve

Right sleeve

C

Left front

Right front

D

2. MAKE THE CUTS

2a. With the main fabric, cut the back piece. It will measure A by E. In the size shown (medium), it is 27"×27".

2b. Cut 2 sleeves. They will measure B by C.

2c. Cut the 2 front panels. Together they should measure about ⅔ the length of A (or D) by E.

2d. With the contrasting fabric, cut three 24"×2" strips for the back elastic casing and ties.

3. IRON THE FABRIC AND SEW THE TUBES

3a. Ironing is key to preparing the fabric for sewing. Iron all your cut fabric pieces well.

3b. Iron each of the contrasting fabric strips in half, wrong sides facing, and sew along the cut edges. Turn inside out with a loop turner or safety pin. If you don't have a loop turner, attach the safety pin to one side of the tube's open edge and push it carefully back through the tube to turn it inside out. Do this for all 3 tubes and then iron them flat.

4. SEW THE BACK AND FRONT

4a. Fold over the top and bottom of the back piece ¾" to the wrong side of the fabric and press. Sew these down with a straight stitch ½" from the edge.

4b. Hem the open edges of the front pieces (right side of left piece and left side of right piece) after folding the edges over twice and pressing thoroughly each time.

4c. Pin the front pieces (with wrong sides facing) to the top of the back piece, with hemmed edges facing the center and raw edges lined up to the right and left sides of the piece. Sew across the top edge.

5. SEW THE SLEEVES

5a. Fold over the open (wrist) edge of the sleeve pieces 1" to the wrong side of the fabric and press. Sew them with a straight stitch and a ½" seam allowance.

5b. Fold the sleeve pieces in half lengthwise, wrong sides facing, and press. Sew them with a straight stitch and a ½" seam allowance.

6. ATTACH SLEEVES

6a. Open up the front and back pieces and place them on the table, right side down. Align the fold line you pressed into the center of each sleeve piece with the hem at the top of the shoulder, where the back and front pieces come together, and pin into place.

6b. Sew across the sleeves, attaching them to the body piece.

6c. Fold the pieces over at the top shoulder seam with right sides facing and pin the side seam and sleeves closed. Starting at the wrist opening, sew the sleeves closed, then complete the underarm sleeve. Repeat on the other side.

6d. Notch the fabric at the underarm to eliminate bulk and make it easier to move the arm.

6e. Turn the yukata right side out and iron well.

7. MAKE ELASTIC AND TIES

7a. Thread the elastic through 1 of the contrasting fabric tubes, fold the edges on 1 tube end to the inside, and line up the elastic near the opening. Sew across the tube opening several times, making sure the elastic is fully caught inside.

7b. Stretch the elastic out through the open end and, using a wide basting stitch, sew down the center of the tube lengthwise to secure the stretched elastic. Turn the remaining open side of the tube to the inside and stitch across to seal. Remove basting stitches.

7c. Pin the fabric-encased elastic into place at the outside center back. To determine placement, with the yukata on, find the spot in the small of your back that corresponds to your waist, or just a little higher. You want the elastic to fall in the natural curve of your back.

7d. Sew the elastic tube down on both sides lengthwise, slightly stretched, so that it will gather the back of the jacket.

7e. Make the side ties by folding the open ends of the 2 remaining tubes to the interior and stitching across to seal. Stitch the left side tie into place on the left side of the elastic tube, and attach the button to the other end. Stitch the right side tie to the right side of the elastic tube and knot it several times to create a loose chain that's just big enough to accommodate your chosen button.

7f. The length of your ties will depend on your waist measurement, but 12" each is typical. You can adjust this to suit your preferences.

FINISH ☒

The Pillow Book: Over 25 simple-to-sew patterns for every room and every mood

Designing yukata-wear isn't Shannon Okey's only talent. Her latest book, *The Pillow Book* (Chronicle Books, $24.95), is filled with all kinds of chic and playful projects. Some of her standouts include an elegant suede overlapping "mermaid scales" pillow, a quilt-style patchwork pillow made from fabric scraps, and a large tufted velvet floor cushion that would add oomph to any room. Beautifully shot, her use of bold colors and stylish fabrics make her easy-to-follow instructions irresistible.
—*Carla Sinclair*

ROCK 'N' ROLL SPEAKERS

By Syuzi Pakhchyan

Excerpted from Craft's new book
FASHIONING TECHNOLOGY
by Syuzi Pakhchyan

BUILD A SET OF STYLISH PORTABLE SPEAKERS THAT FLIP ON AND OFF.

Photography by Syuzi Pakhchyan; illustrations by Tim Lillis

▶▶ Whether you're at a Bangkok hostel or backpacking in Goa, you can rock out to your favorite tunes with these portable Rock 'n' Roll Speakers, a set of customizable, low-fi travel speakers that allow you to take your music everywhere.

The speakers are driven by a simple power amplifier circuit and a tilt switch. With a simple flip, these portable speakers are switched on and off: when both speakers are visible the speakers are on, and when only one speaker is visible they're off. Powered by a 9V battery, the Rock 'n' Roll Speakers are the perfect compact travel companions for adventurous jet-setters.

If you like this project, you'll find dozens more like it in CRAFT's new book, *Fashioning Technology* (buy it at craftzine.com/fashiontech).

» Launched in 1979, the Sony Walkman was originally designed for Sony co-chairman Akio Morita, who wanted to listen to his favorite operas while traveling.

» A speaker is essentially just an electromagnet that jiggles a paper cone, turning electrical energy into sound.

» The song "Leaving On A Jet Plane" was written in 1967 by John Denver, in an airport while he waited for a delayed flight.

Syuzi Pakhchyan is an interaction designer, robotics instructor, and professional tinkerer working and residing in L.A. Her studio and R&P (Research and Play) facility, SparkLab, fuses design with entertainment. fashioningtech.com

WHAT YOU'LL NEED

[A] Glue

[B] Wire cutters

[C] White spray paint (optional)

[D] 9V battery

[E] 16" clear heat-shrink tubing ¼" diameter

[F] Needlenose pliers

[G] Wire strippers

[H] 18"×18" mat board

[I] 18"×18" decorative paper or fabric for speaker cover

[J] Scissors

[K] Hot glue gun

[L] Drill (optional)

[M] 8Ω speakers (2)

[N] 12" heat-shrink tubing ⅙" diameter

[O] Tilt switch nonmetallic

[P] 10Ω resistor

[Q] 220µF and 0.05µF capacitors

[R] LM386 audio amplifier IC

[S] 10KΩ trimpot (variable resistor)

[T] Utility knife

[U] 2"×2" perf board

[V] Variety of jumper wires or solid wire

[W] 9V battery connector

[X] Audio plug

[Y] Double-sided tape

[Z] 1" hook and loop square

[NOT SHOWN]

12" piece of conductive fabric tape

6' stranded wire

Marker

Photograph by Sam Murphy

▶▶ USE SIMPLE ELECTRONICS TO MAKE TRAVEL SPEAKERS

Time: 3 Hours Complexity: Medium (Difficult for novices)

1. MAKE THE FORM

1a. Using the template at craftzine.com/07/speakers, trace the pattern on mat board and cut out the form.

1b. You can optionally customize the speakers by covering the form with decorative paper or fabric. Using the appropriate adhesive for your chosen material, glue it directly on top of the cut form, wrapping the edges into the inside of the form. Fold the form along the score lines.

1c. Using spray paint, spray the speakers until they are evenly coated.

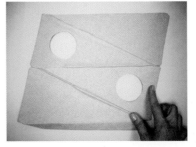

NOTE: If you choose not to cover the form with paper or fabric, you could also paint it.

2. MAKE THE SWITCH

2a. Cut and strip both ends of two 1½" pieces of stranded wire. Next, cut two 1" pieces of heat-shrink tubing.

2b. Grab the tilt switch. Wrap one of the stripped ends of a wire onto a switch lead, and solder. Slip the heat-shrink tubing over the connection. Using a heat gun or blow dryer, shrink the tubing. Repeat for the second lead. Then cut the positive, red wire of the connector ½" from the top. Strip the cut ends.

2c. Next, cut two ¼" pieces of heat-shrink tubing. Slip the pieces of heat-shrink over one of the switch wires. Twist the 2 wires from the switch and battery connector together and solder. Slip the tubing over the connection and shrink. Repeat, connecting the second switch wire to the loose, cut wire from the battery connector.

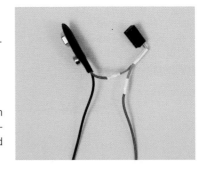

3. MAKE THE PLUG

3a. Cut and strip both ends of three 16" pieces of stranded wire. Twist the ends.

3b. Remove the audio plug cover. Slip the wires through the right, left, and center terminals of the plug and twist them into place. Solder.

3c. Cut two 1" pieces of heat-shrink tubing. Slip them over the right and left terminals and shrink.

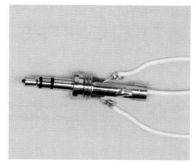

3d. Using a black marker, mark the bottom of the wire leading from the center terminal. This will be the ground wire. Slip clear ¼"-diameter heat-shrink tubing over all 3 wires. Do not shrink. Replace the plug cover.

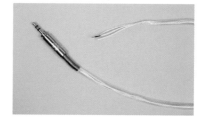

4. BUILD THE CIRCUIT

If you've never built a circuit on a perforated board before, go to craftzine.com/07/speakers for more detailed information on how to use a perf board.

The illustration at right shows how the components of the circuit are connected to each other.

NOTE: This schematic is not a direct translation of how the circuit will be played out on the perforated board.

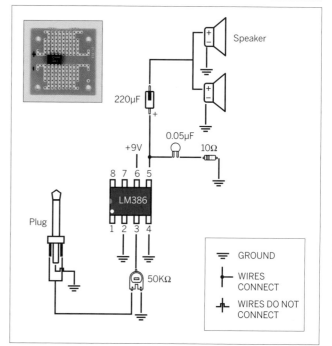

Illustration by Syuzi Pakhchyan

4a. Grab the LM386 audio amplifier IC. Locate the notch and dot. The pins on the IC are numbered starting counterclockwise from the dot, as in the facing illustration. Using a perf board designed with standard IC and component spacing, place the IC in the center of the perf board. Designate a row for power (+) and a row for ground (−) by marking the assigned holes.

4b. Using jumper wire, connect pin 6 to power, pin 4 to ground, and pin 2 to ground.

4c. From pin 5, a 0.05µF capacitor must connect to a 10Ω resistor, which then has to be grounded. Also from pin 5, a 220µF capacitor must be connected. Connect a wire from pin 5 and jump it 2 rows over (red wire). Connect 1 lead of the 0.05µF capacitor to that row and the other lead 2 rows over. To hold the capacitor temporarily in place, bend the leads flush to the bottom of the board. Connect 1 lead of the resistor to the second lead of the 0.05µF capacitor, and the second lead of the resistor to a separate row. Using jumper wire, connect the second lead of the resistor to ground.

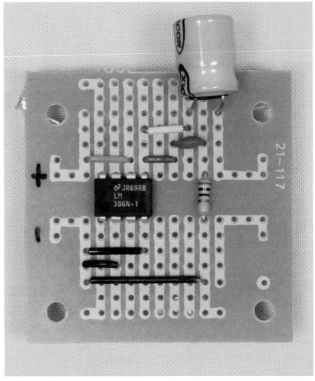

4d. Connect another wire from pin 5 and jump it 3 rows over (yellow wire). Connect the positive lead of the 220µF capacitor (the lead without the black band) to that row, and connect its other lead 2 rows over.

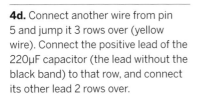

4e. Ultimately, the middle lead of the 10K trimpot must be connected to pin 3, with one of its outer leads connected to ground while the other is connected to the input of the audio plug. Start by connecting a wire from pin 3 and jump it 3 rows over (blue wire). Connect the middle lead of the trimpot to the same row. Connect one of the leads to ground.

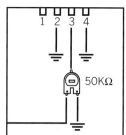

4f. Cut and strip six 8" pieces of stranded wire. Take 2 wires and connect them to the negative lead of the 220µF capacitor (Figure A). These wires will be the positive wires of the speakers.

Grab another 2 wires and connect them to ground (Figure B). Using a black marker, mark these 2 ground wires.

Next, connect a wire to the second (not grounded) lead of the trimpot (Figure C). This wire will lead to the plug input.

Grab the last wire. Connect it to ground (Figure D). This wire will lead to the grounded side of the audio plug.

4g. Take the battery connector-switch piece, and insert the red wire into the power row and the negative into ground. Now grab the speakers. Slip the positive speaker wires from the board into the positive terminals of the speakers and the negative wires into the negative terminals. Twist, securing them in place.

4h. Carefully review all connection points in the circuit. When everything is connected properly, solder all components into place, and solder the connections at the speaker terminals. Don't solder the audio plug yet — you'll add it later.

5. ATTACH THE SPEAKERS AND CIRCUIT TO THE FORM

5a. On the form, pierce a hole in the center of the back triangle (the one without the fold). Use a drill if you have one. Next, using hot glue, attach the speakers in place. Position the circuit on the front triangle and glue it securely to the mat board. Slide the plug-wire piece through the drilled hole.

5b. Cut two 1" pieces of heat-shrink tubing. Slip the heat-shrink over the ground wire of the plug. Wrap the ground wire of the plug to the ground wire coming from the circuit. Solder and shrink the tubing. Repeat for the plug's 2 input wires, attaching both input wires from the plug to the corresponding wire on the trimpot.

5c. Locate an ideal position for the 9V battery on the top triangle of the form. Using a piece of sticky hook and loop tape, attach the battery to the top triangle. Using hot glue, adhere corresponding strips of hook and loop on opposite ends of the inside of the form and the top of the fold.

5d. Connect a 9V battery to the battery connector and plug in your portable music player.

5e. Determine the angle at which the tilt switch switches on. Hot-glue the tilt switch in the appropriate position so that it's "on" when the front of the speaker is facing forward (when you can see both speakers) and "off" when the front speaker is facing down (when you can only see one speaker).

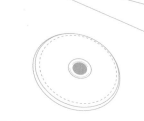
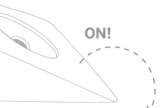

ON!

OFF!

FINISH ☒

Illustration by Katie Wilson

CHIC BATIK

By Teresa Mak

USE TRADITIONAL WAX AND DYES ON FABRICS TO PAINT A MODERN PICTURE.

▶▶ The history and customs of many cultures have been expressed through textiles for centuries. In Southeast Asia, batiking has been the medium for fabric design for almost 2,000 years. While in Bali, I had the opportunity to learn about batiking fabrics, and though most of the designs there showcase mythical themes, I wanted to make something more personal. Sitting on a grass mat under a mango tree, amongst the roving chickens and dogs, I created my own personal history through batiking.

Traditionally, the technique entails using wax to block the dyes used to color the fabric. I used wax and shades of cold-water dye on cotton fabric.

» A *kebaya* is a traditional Southeast Asian blouse typically worn with a batik print sarong.

» For a long time in Indonesia, only the Sultan of Yogyakarta's immediate family was allowed to wear batik clothing, which bore the royal *kawung* motif.

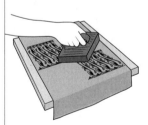

» Developed in the mid-19th century, copper stamps called cap (pronounced "chop") allow for faster wax application so that batik prints can be easily mass-produced.

Teresa Mak's interest in textiles began early, when her mum was a seamstress in downtown Toronto. Based in Los Angeles, she experiments with natural dyes and dye techniques on large bolts of unraveling cloth. Her crafty pursuits can be found at tallwheat.blogspot.com.

Photography by Teresa Mak; illustrations by Tim Lillis

WHAT YOU'LL NEED

[A] Iron

[B] Small cooking pots

[C] Procion MX fiber
reactive cold water dyes
I used Yellow, Turquoise, Fire
Engine Red, Brown Rose,
Red, and Black.

[D] Glass containers
to hold approximately
1c of liquid

[E] Cotton muslin or
broadcloth 100% cotton,
approximately 1yd

[F] Scissors

[G] Staple gun and staples

[H] Pencil

[I] Stretcher bars or
wooden frame, 20"×24"

[J] Brushes various sizes

[K] Measuring tape

[L] Detergent with no
dyes or brighteners
such as Synthrapol

[M] Newspaper

**FROM AN ART SUPPLY OR
SPECIALTY DYE STORE:**

[N] Tjantings (tools for
applying wax) various sizes

[O] Sodium carbonate
in powder form

[P] Batik paraffin wax

[Q] Beeswax

[NOT SHOWN]

Urea powder form

Noniodized salt

Rubber gloves

Screwdriver

Plastic garbage bag

Paper towels

Measuring cup and
measuring spoons

⏩ DESIGN, APPLY, AND DYE A CUSTOM IMAGE

Time: 1 Week Complexity: Medium

1. PREPARE THE FABRIC

1a. Using a cold water cycle, wash the cotton fabric using Synthrapol or a natural detergent without dyes or brighteners. Hang to dry.

1b. Measure the amount of fabric you'll use by laying it out on a flat surface and placing the stretcher frame on top. Using scissors and a measuring tape, cut the muslin so that there's at least a 2" overlap on each side of the stretcher frame. Using a 20"×24" frame, your fabric should measure approximately 24"×28". Remove the frame and iron the fabric to eliminate any wrinkles.

2. STRETCH THE FABRIC

2a. Lay the fabric on a flat surface, and place the stretcher frame in the middle. Starting on 1 side of the frame, fold the fabric over and staple it down at the center. Add a staple to the left and right of the center staple, approximately 2" apart.

2b. On the side opposite to where you started, fold and staple the center in the same way, keeping the fabric taut. Rotate the frame, and staple the 2 remaining sides the same way.

2c. When each side is securely fastened, continue rotating and stapling outward from the centers, pulling the fabric taut and placing each new staple opposite the last. Staple until you reach the corners of the frame.

2d. Trim the excess fabric from the sides, so that the fabric is about even with the inner edges of the frame. Staple each corner down with a single staple.

3. SKETCH A PICTURE

With a pencil, sketch a picture onto the fabric. I chose to sketch a picture of my surroundings in Bali. It's helpful to note somewhere the colors you'd like to see associated with the elements in your picture.

4. APPLY THE WAX

The batik process involves applying wax and dye to fabric in succession. Wax is applied first, to block off white areas. The cloth is then dyed, and then a second application of wax is made to block out areas of this dyed color. The fabric is continually waxed and dyed with additional colors, until it's fully colored.

Although traditional batik is dyed in a vat, for this project, we'll apply the dye to the fabric using a brush. Steps 4–6 will be repeated in succession until the cloth is fully colored.

The following steps are essential to the batik process. We'll apply wax to the fabric for each color we use in the dyeing process. Allow some time to get comfortable with handling hot wax and using the various tools.

WAXES & WAX TOOLS

A *tjanting* (pronounced chahn-ting) is a traditional tool used for applying hot wax to fabric, available in various line widths. I use one to draw lines and dots.

A cheap **natural bristle brush** is also helpful for applying hot wax to large areas of fabric. Be sure to use natural bristles, as synthetic brushes may melt in the hot wax.

Different waxes produce different resist effects on fabric. For this project, we'll use beeswax and a batik wax made of paraffin. Apply each wax, one after another, and use separate brushes for each of them.

Beeswax is yellow in color, honey-scented, and produces a thin, flexible film on the fabric. I use beeswax to draw outlines of shapes and objects, and to block out large areas of solid color.

Paraffin wax is white in color and more brittle than beeswax, so it cracks easily, producing a veined, crackle effect, which I like to use on larger areas of fabric.

4a. Melt the beeswax in a small pot over an electric burner. If the wax begins to smoke, quickly remove the pot from the burner. You need at least 1" of melted wax in the pot so that you have enough for your batik tools to dip into. For paraffin wax, use a separate pot. Paraffin wax has a lower smoking point than beeswax, so make sure you keep a close watch on the paraffin to avoid flare-ups!

4b. When the wax is almost melted, place your tjanting in the wax to heat up. You'll notice that a crust of wax will form, indicating that the tjanting is too cold. When your tjanting is sufficiently warm and ready to use, no solid wax should be visible on any part of the tool. Dip the tjanting into the pot and collect wax in the reservoir. To ensure that no cold wax remains in the reservoir of the tjanting, pour the wax out into the pot, then continue to collect and pour out the wax a few more times. Repeat this step each time you collect wax from the pot.

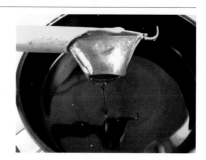

4c. Fill the tjanting reservoir with melted wax, wiping the side of the tjanting against the side of the pot to remove excess wax. Use a paper towel to catch any drips.

4d. Test that the wax is hot enough by drawing a few lines on a piece of newspaper. When the applied wax is translucent in color and seeps through the newsprint onto the other side, the wax is ready. If the wax is opaque and sits on top of the fabric, then the wax is too cold. Continue heating and testing the wax until the applied wax is translucent.

4e. When the wax is hot enough, use the tjanting to apply it to the pencil sketches you drew earlier on the stretched fabric. Apply to both the front and back. A brush can also be used to apply wax to larger areas of the fabric. Warm the brush first in the wax before applying.

NOTE: Be sure to apply wax to both the front and the back of your sketch.

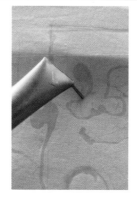

4f. Allow an hour for the wax to fully harden. If you used paraffin wax, use your index finger to apply light pressure to the hardened wax. The wax will crackle with applied pressure.

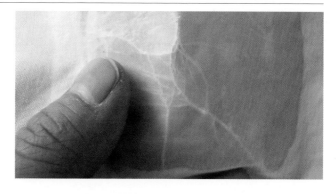

5. MIX AND APPLY THE DYE

5a. Don your rubber gloves when handling dyes and solutions. The dye is only good within a few hours of mixing, so only mix the dye you're going to use at the time.

To make each dye solution, combine the following:
1tsp urea
½Tbsp noniodized salt
½Tbsp sodium carbonate
1–2tsp Procion MX dye (see table at right)

In a glass jar, add ¼c of boiling water to the dry ingredients, and stir until everything is fully dissolved.

COLOR	DYES USED
Yellow	1tsp Yellow MX-4G
Blue	1tsp Turquoise MX-G
Light Red	1tsp Fire Engine Red MX-BRA
Dark Red	1tsp Brown Rose MX-5BR
Black	1tsp Warm Black MX-CWNA
	¼tsp Black MX-K/Jet Black 150
	¼tsp Brown Rose MX-5BR
	¼tsp Fire Engine Red MX-BRA

5b. With a clean paintbrush, apply the dye solution to sections of the fabric that you want colored. If you're mixing 2 primary colors, apply one color first, then apply the other color on top using a separate brush. Allow the fabric to dry before applying more wax.

6. REPEAT THE WAX-AND-DYE PROCESS

Steps 4 and 5 are repeated for each color of dye. For my batik painting, I used yellow, blue, light red, dark red, and black dyes.

» First I applied wax to the stretched fabric, allowed it to harden, then painted yellow dye on the mango trees and the mangos. Then I applied wax to sections that remain yellow, and applied blue dye to the foliage and mangos to make them green.

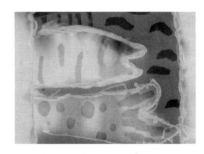

» For the section that required several different colors, I initially outlined the painting in beeswax on white fabric, then painted on yellow dye, then blue dye, which results in green. I then applied beeswax on top of the green to add water accents.

» After the beeswax hardened, I painted light red dye to make brown, set it outside to dry, then made another application of beeswax to highlight brown water accents and light red fish scales. After that hardened, I painted dark red dye on the borders. Once dry, I applied paraffin to the borders. And when the paraffin wax hardened, I applied pressure to it to create a crackle effect.

» Finally, I painted on the black dye, which seeped underneath the cracked paraffin. The black dye also contributed to the black accents found in the fish.

⊞ For a table illustrating the coloring process, go to craftzine.com/07/batik.

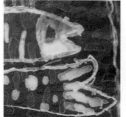
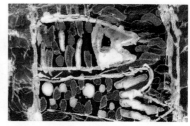

7. SET AND RINSE THE DYE

7a. Allow the dye to react. With the last application of black dye, check that the stretched fabric is damp with black dye. Wrap the damp frame and fabric in a plastic garbage bag. Roll down the opening to ensure that the bag remains sealed and the frame and fabric stay moist. Place the bagged frame and fabric in a warm place for 12–24 hours.

7b. Rinse the fabric. With the fabric still on the frame, put your rubber gloves on and rinse the fabric with cold water until the water runs clear. Then follow with a rinse in hot water. Thoroughly air-dry both the fabric and frame.

8. REMOVE THE WAX

8a. Pry the staples out of the frame with a screwdriver, then remove the fabric. Then sandwich the fabric between 2 layers of paper towels and newspaper. The paper towels should be closest to the fabric.

8b. With a hot iron adjusted to the cotton setting, iron slowly over the newspaper and paper towels until the wax melts out of the fabric and is absorbed by the paper. Change the paper towels and newspapers frequently. When most of the wax has been removed from the fabric, the fabric should feel slightly stiff.

You can now showcase your batik painting by framing it, or by stretching it back onto the frame you used to make it.

SPECIAL THANKS to my teacher, Nioman, in Bali for teaching me how to batik.

NOTE: An alternate method is to boil the wax out of the fabric using soap flakes and boiling water. I find that this technique, while better at removing wax from the fabric, tends to cause the dye to fade out of the fabric.

FINISH ☒

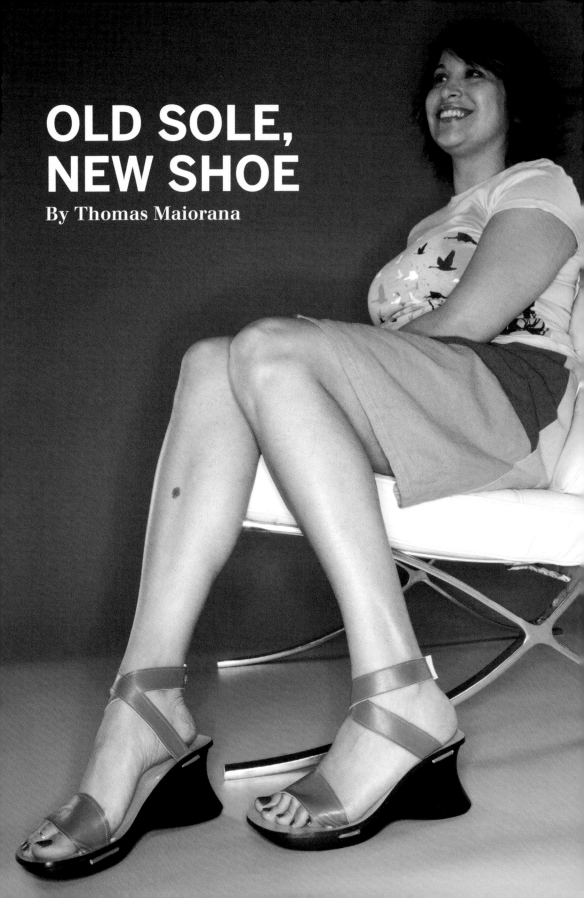

OLD SOLE,
NEW SHOE

By Thomas Maiorana

MAKE SUMMERTIME FOOTWEAR THAT ALLOWS YOU TO SWAP COLORS, FABRICS, AND STYLES.

➤➤ You'd be hard-pressed to find an accessory infused with more passion and personality than shoes. Despite this, we're offered a relatively limited number of styles and models. Unless you're super rich (unlikely) or a shoe-maker (even less likely) you probably haven't considered custom footwear. However, making your own shoes is easier than you think.

I'm talking about creating new, interchangeable uppers that reflect your creative vision, from material choice to pattern. By cannibalizing the soles from pre-existing footwear, you can make a pair of strappy shoes with unlimited styles that you can swap out as fashion sees fit.

» The average American woman has 19 pairs of shoes, but wears only four pairs regularly.

» Old tires can be recycled to make soles for shoes.

» In the 80s, Units were a line of clothing that sold modular one-size-fits-all pieces that could be mixed and matched in different combinations to create new outfits.

Thomas Maiorana is a creative strategist based in San Francisco. He first developed this way of making shoes while getting a master's degree in design from Stanford University. He's always happy to share new ways to create interesting footwear. tom@bootyamor.org

Photograph by Garry McLeod; illustrations by Tim Lillis

OPEN SOURCE SHOES
Making a Case to Go Modular

When I mention that I make shoes, I often get the same response: "Oh my God, can you make me some? I'm a total shoe addict!" If you're anything like me, you've had fantastic visions of creating your own boots, platforms, wingtips ...

But very few of us actually turn these ideas into reality. Making shoes isn't easy. The fact that the process is surrounded with an aura of mystery doesn't help either. As a result, custom shoes are only available to those with the means to pay a shoemaker hundreds of dollars per pair. The rest of us must search through a sea of mediocre, mass-produced footwear. This needs to change.

We can start by taking some lessons from open source models of software development. How? We're going to cannibalize existing shoes, make them modular, and minimize the risk of experimentation.

Cannibalize

We start by cannibalizing the most complicated part of the shoe — the sole. The sole provides support and cushioning to the foot's complex structure of bones, joints, muscles, and tendons. Since most shoe companies spend quite a bit of time and money working out issues of construction, materials, and support, we can benefit from their hard work by using existing soles as the platform from which we can build.

Go Modular

Currently, almost all shoes are constructed by gluing the upper (the part that covers your foot) to the soles. Once connected, it's nearly impossible to remove these parts from one another without doing damage.

But if we construct shoes to be modular, then the uppers could be removed from the sole without destroying either part. Straps could be swapped as easily as Lego bricks. In the open source world, developing code in this way allows software developers to distribute a workload in manageable sections. Since the shoe is a complicated object, it will be much easier for us to build if we break the object into discrete elements.

Minimize Risk

Because the whole is broken into interchangeable parts, failure in one realm doesn't bring the whole endeavor down. I experienced this firsthand when I made shoes in the traditional way.

I had measured the foot, drafted patterns, cut final materials, sewn them together, and finally glued the upper to the sole. But somewhere in there I made a mistake. When my girlfriend tried on the shoes, they were three sizes too big. Mistakes in a modular system are far less costly. You simply rebuild the part rather than the whole shoe.

By letting companies do the hard stuff for us, we can start making custom shoes much faster and cheaper than if we had to build the whole object. And because we only need to make part of the shoe, we can make custom shoes for less than $20. The pair I built here cost less than $15, and I wasn't even cutting corners.

However, I don't make shoes because it's inexpensive. I do it because I love bringing my ideas to life. Building modular shoes makes this process much more enjoyable because it allows me to make changes and improve a design even as I'm making the shoe. These flexible construction methods should empower you to make daring, shocking, or surprising shoes. So start building. Your shoes are waiting.

WHAT YOU'LL NEED

[A] Old or cheap shoes

[B] ⅛"×1' acrylic rod
or wood dowel

[C] X-Acto knife

[D] Rolling cutter
or scissors

[E] Contact cement

[F] 1'×2' piece of leather,
strong fabric, or mate-
rial of your choice for the
uppers. Get a second piece if
you're making a lining too.

[G] 3'×3' piece of felt for
prototyping material

[NOT SHOWN]

Sewing machine

Pliers

Fine-tooth saw or Dremel
rotary tool for cutting the
rod or dowel

Shoe last or a patient friend

Baby powder

Small piece of thin fabric
for dusting the pattern

START

▶▶ USING SOLES AS YOUR CANVAS, DESIGN A PAIR OF SHOES ... AGAIN AND AGAIN

Time: **1 Day** Complexity: **Medium**

1. GO SHOPPING

Shop for a pair of shoes. You can find cheap shoes with good soles at thrift stores. Look for shoes with a nice shape, a leather footbed, and the right type of soles. Most pumps and heels will do. You should feel some resistance when you try to bend the shoe with your hands. The shoes I've selected have 3 elements that make them ideal: the leather footbed is fairly thick; the sole is at least ½" off the ground; and the footbed has a slight overhang. The shoe you choose has more of an impact on this project than any other decision you make.

2. CUT THE UPPER OFF

Once you've got your shoes, take a deep breath and start cutting. Remove any part of the shoe that sticks up from the sole. I recommend using an X-Acto knife. Take your time and make multiple passes.

3. CUT STRAP SLOTS INTO THE SOLES

3a. Since the sole is going to be the base for any variations you make, take your time as you use an X-Acto knife to cut the slots that you'll later run the straps through. Start by noting the location of the elements you just removed. I find that most shoes have a way of telling me where they want the straps to be.

For these shoes, I used 2 of the holes as endpoints, and the slots fell just forward of the ball of the foot and just forward of the heel. Each slot should be less than 1½" long and approximately ⅛" wide. Be careful to leave about ¼" between the slot and the edge of the sole. Any closer than that and you risk tear-out.

Photography by Thomas Maiorana

3b. Once you've cut the slots into the top, cut slots on each side of the sole, just below the footbed and below the top slots you've just made. You're creating passageways between the top and side slots. Remove the excess material and clean out the passageway. Repeat this process on the other 3 locations.

NOTE: There are many ways you can attach the uppers to the soles, but I've found this one to be very simple. Once you've made your slots, sew a loop at the ends of each strap, pass the strap through a slot, then insert a pin into the loop. This method allows you to assemble and reassemble different looks with the same pair of soles.

4. PLAN YOUR DESIGN AND MAKE A PATTERN

4a. Now that you've prepared the raw sole, you'll want to plan your first shoe. Create a 3D sketch by cutting strips of felt and running them through the slots. With this cheaper fabric, you can test your patterns and get a feel for the ways in which the straps will cover your foot. During this stage, feel free to cut the felt at will, mark it up, and see how it looks. If you screw up, cut another strip and do it again.

4b. Patterns will vary depending on the shoes you cannibalize, so the felt will help you decide how to cut the final materials. Pull the felt through the slots so that it starts to look like the final shoe. In this case, I used a last to measure, but a real foot works just as well. If you're making shoes for yourself, try to enlist someone to pull the felt tightly around your foot while you're standing in the shoes. You can do it on your own, but there's quite a bit of Twister involved. Once the felt feels right, have your assistant mark the felt just below the sole.

4c. Remove the felt from the sole and trim it neatly. This is your pattern. Make sure to account for the allowance you'll need to create the loop in the fabric. Then mark L and R on each side. Be sure to double-check this part. I can't tell you how many times I've made 2 lefts. It stops being funny after the first time.

5. CUT YOUR PATTERN

Lay your material wrong-side up and lay your pattern on it. Use thin fabric and baby powder to create a little duster. Dab the pattern's edge all around. Then pull up the felt for a ghosted pattern. Cut it out with the sharp tool of your choice. If you're backing your upper, repeat with a second piece of material, being careful to flip your pattern. The backing is the mirror image of the upper, but it doesn't have the loop allowance.

Illustration by Thomas Maiorana

6. ASSEMBLE THE BACKING AND THE UPPER

6a. If using fabric, sew everything together as you would a garment. First fold the loop allowance over, leaving enough room for the rod (approximately ¼"). Now sew along the edge of the allowance, enclosing the loop. Then sew the upper and backing together. If there's a lot of stretch, you'll need to sandwich an extra layer between them.

6b. If using leather, glue the pieces with a thin layer of contact cement. (Since you can't pin leather, this is how you connect it before sewing.) Then sew the cemented pieces together. If using garment-weight leather, you may be able to sew it on your own machine, but be careful. Work up to it by practicing on a single layer first. Get a feel for how your machine is responding. If it's not having trouble, continue, but if it's straining, stop sewing. It'll be much cheaper to bring the pieces to a shoe repair shop or a dry cleaner that does tailoring. You should now have pieces that look like the photo at right. Trim off the excess backing.

NOTE: Repair shops have industrial sewing machines. If you choose this route, give clear instructions and negotiate a price.

7. MEASURE AND CUT THE PIN

With a fine-tooth saw or Dremel tool, cut your rod or dowel to make the pins. Because of the sole flex, try keeping the pin under 2"; I find 1½" or smaller is ideal. The pin should be about ⅛"–¼" longer than the groove you've cut into the sole. This overlap keeps your strap from coming out. Once you have the correct length, sand the ends of the wood or acrylic to remove any sharp edges.

NOTE: I suggest using an acrylic rod since it's light and easy to cut, and it slides through material easily. With that said, I used wood dowels for this project, because they were easier to find.

8. ASSEMBLE THE SHOE

Slip the end of the strap through the slot in the front of the shoe. Once it's through, slide the pin into the loop at the end of the strap and pull the strap so the pin is snug against the sole. Now connect the other side of the front strap and do the same at the heel.

FINISH ✕

Photography by Sam Murphy; cross-stitched by Caroline Murphy

Designer Dots

Create your own cross-stitch pattern with a perfectly pixelated digital image. BY CHARLES PLATT

Almost all printed photographs are made of dots. Look closely in magazines, on inkjet pages, or even on billboards, and you can see the dots — but as you move farther away, your eyes perceive the image created by the dots.

Here's a project that applies this optical phenomenon to the ancient art of cross-stitching. Close up you'll see the stitches, but at arm's length the stitches will seem to merge to form a photographic image. All you need to make this happen are a little patience, traditional cross-stitching supplies, a digital camera, and an image editing program such as Photoshop.

Fig. A: Start with any photographic-quality artwork containing a good range of colors or shades, and not too much fine detail.

Fig. B: Using image processing software, "pixelate" the artwork so that each pixel will represent 1 cross-stitch.

Materials

» **Computer**
» **Image processing software, such as Adobe Photoshop** which is what I've used here.

 SOFTWARE

The most recent version of Photoshop is expensive, but you can buy older versions on eBay for $30 to $60. **NOTE: eBay does not knowingly permit the sale of bootleg software.** These instructions will work with Photoshop 6 or later. Open-source image-editing software for Mac, Windows, and Linux is available free from gimpshop.com, with menus much like those of Photoshop, although we cannot guarantee that the instructions here will function identically.

1. Choose a picture.

For best results, it should not contain a lot of fine detail, and it's helpful to select an image with a single-color background if possible. Portraits are ideal. I chose a picture of a pigeon (Figure A).

2. Paint out the background.

You have to isolate your subject visually from the background if it's not already. Open your picture in Photoshop. I used the Eyedropper tool to sample a light gray in the pigeon's wing, then applied that color to the background with the Paintbrush tool. Don't worry about painting around very thin lines, which will disappear anyway.

3. Choose your image size.

For a starter project I suggest a stitched area about 5" wide on 16-thread-count fabric. This means you'll be sewing 80 stitches per line. Since 1 stitch will represent each pixel, you need to convert your image to 80 pixels per line.

In Photoshop, choose Image ⇒ Image Size from the menu bar. In the dialog that opens, make sure the Resample Image option is checked near the bottom. Enter 80 pixels for the image width. Ignore the height and other data fields; click OK. Your image will shrink to almost nothing, so choose View ⇒ Fit on Screen from the menu bar to see the pixels (Figure B).

C D

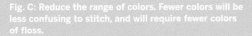

Fig. C: Reduce the range of colors. Fewer colors will be less confusing to stitch, and will require fewer colors of floss.

Fig. D: Add intensity, saturation, or contrast to your image to compensate for the limited color palette.

4. Preview the effect.

Move a few feet away from your video monitor. If the image doesn't adapt well, try a different photograph.

5. Choose a palette.

Your computer displays images in millions of colors, but for cross-stitching we want to use only a few colors of floss. From the menu bar, choose Image ⇒ Mode ⇒ Indexed Color. In the dialog box that opens, for the Palette option choose Local (Adaptive); for the Forced option choose None; for the Dither option choose None; and for the Colors option try entering various numbers from 4 upward.

You should be able to preview the results while the dialog box is open. Eight colors were sufficient for the pigeon. Click OK when you're happy with the result (Figure C).

6. Add saturation.

When you reduced the number of colors in Step 5, each one became a compromise. This is like mixing many colors in a paint box: they tend to get muddy. From the menu bar, choose Image ⇒ Adjust ⇒ Hue/Saturation and play with the sliders to make your picture more interesting (Figure D).

7. Create swatches.

You'll be able to keep track of your colors more easily if you make a row of swatches in a blank area of your image (Figure E). Using the Eyedropper tool, click in an area of your photo, then use the Marquee tool to create a small square. From the menu bar, choose Edit ⇒ Fill and click the Foreground Color option. Repeat this procedure for all the colors in your photo.

8. Convert back to RGB.

Convert your image from Indexed Color back to RGB color by selecting Image ⇒ Mode ⇒ RGB Color. This will make subsequent steps easier.

9. Print the image.

We want your printed version to be the same size as your cross-stitched version, but your printer may be unpredictable if you try to print only 16 pixels per inch. We'll keep it happy by "upsampling" the image.

Again choose Image ⇒ Image Size from the menu bar. In the dialog box that opens, for the Resolution option, enter 160 if you're going to use 16-count fabric, or enter 140 if you're going to use 14-count fabric, and so on. Don't click OK yet!

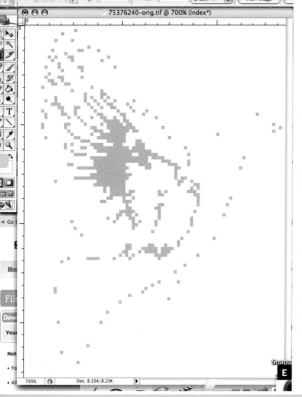

E F

Fig. E: Create color swatches (samples) to reduce confusion and to help you create color separations as in Step 11.

Fig. F: The final design, completely cross-stitched and ready to fly!

Now change the width from 80 to 800 pixels, and near the bottom of the dialog box where it shows you options to Resample Image, choose the Nearest Neighbor option (otherwise, your nice sharp pixels will get blurred). Now click OK, and you should be able to print your image full-size without problems.

10. Add a grid.

You'll need a grid (like graph paper) to help you count stitches. The easiest way is to print your image and draw a grid by hand, in colored pen. Some people find it easiest to use 1 grid square per pixel. I like using 1 grid line per 5 pixels to reduce the workload.

11. Print color separations.

To avoid confusion, you can make a separate print of each color (Figure E). First, in the Toolbox, change your background color to white (consult Photoshop Help if you aren't sure how to do this). Save your work. Now select the Magic Wand tool, set its tolerance to 0, uncheck its Anti-Aliased option, and uncheck its Contiguous option. Use it as follows:

a. Save your art under a new filename.
b. Using the Magic Wand tool, click the first of your swatches. This should select all the instances of

the color that you clicked.
c. Choose Select ⇒ Inverse from the menu bar.
d. Choose Edit ⇒ Cut from the menu bar to remove all the pixels except the ones you selected.
e. Print the page.
f. Choose Edit ⇒ Undo Cut Pixels from the menu bar to restore everything.
g. Choose Select ⇒ Deselect to deselect everything.
h. Repeat Step 11 with a new filename for the next color.

12. Go shopping!

Take your printed pages to a craft store and select floss that matches your color swatches. Note that matching the lightness or darkness of the swatches is more important than matching their exact color.

You've finished the hard part. Next comes the easy part: the stitching. And finally, the fun part, which is when your friends stare at the result and say, "How ever did you do that?"

Charles Platt once majored in mathematics, and is the author of the crafts book *T-Shirting*, published by Franklin Watts.

It's a Small World

Create your own little dominion. BY PATRICIA ZAPATA

I made my first diorama when I was in elementary school, and years later, I *still* think they're fun to make. For me, the best part is that the possibilities are endless. Lately, I've been working with cut paper illustrations, and since my projects are mostly inspired by nature, it's no surprise that I ended up combining those two aspects of my work here.

To get started, go through your old photos, illustrations, and doodles to see what most interests you, then start sketching your scene. You can be as creative as you like when it comes to materials: recycled magazines, swatches of fabric, gift wrap, and small figurines can all be used. Just start collecting and soon you'll have constructed your own little domain.

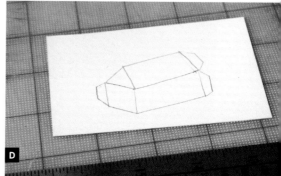

Fig. A: Gather all materials for your diorama and remember to try to use things you already have. Fig. B: If you're using a frame, it's easier to create a stage first. Skip this step if you're using a shoe box.

Fig. C: Create a background that will enhance but not overwhelm the main focus of your diorama. Fig. D: Draw a cabin on an angle to help the illusion of perspective.

Materials

- » **Shadow box frame or shoe box**
- » **Assorted colors of cardstock**
- » **Foamcore board**
- » **Spray adhesive**
- » **Tape, glue, and glue stick**
- » **Bone folder, pencil, X-Acto knife, scissors, ruler, and cutting mat**
- » **Wooden skewers** cut into small lengths
- » **Small deer figurine**

1. Measure the box.

Measure the inside of your shadow box frame. Use these dimensions to cut a stage out of white cardstock that will cover the bottom, back, and sides of your frame (Figure B). Use a bone folder to fold for a nicer finish. If using a shoe box, you can simply build your scene from the back toward the front, without building a stage. When using a box frame with set glass, build your scene first, then slip it into the box.

2. Create the background.

Using the same measurements, create a blue background and attach it to the back and sides of the white cardstock with glue stick or spray adhesive. Don't use too much glue — large quantities may make the paper bubble. Once the blue paper is in place, turn the whole piece over on a clean surface and rub the entire area behind the blue paper so that it sticks evenly to the white background.

3. Make the background trees.

With black cardstock, draw and cut out a scene of trees (Figure C). Glue them to the blue background, turn the whole piece over, and rub as before. I cut 3 pieces each (for the back and sides) of the black and blue papers instead of 1 long piece of each because when the scene is folded and upright the corners may bubble due to the thickness of the paper.

4. Make the cabin.

Draw an outline of the cabin with tabs on 3 sides (Figure D). You'll use these to glue the cabin to the back of the diorama. The cabin is drawn at a slight angle to give an illusion of perspective. Cut out the cabin, then glue on small horizontal pieces of the cut

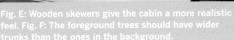

Fig. E: Wooden skewers give the cabin a more realistic feel. Fig. F: The foreground trees should have wider trunks than the ones in the background.

Fig. G: Glue trees to the stage. Don't place them too close to the cabin. Fig. H: Before gluing the second set of trees make sure that the deer fits comfortably. Once everything is dry, the stage and trees are ready for paint.

wooden skewers (use the X-Acto knife or scissors to chop the wood). Cover everything except the tabs. Glue a small black paper triangle to the left end of the cabin (Figure E). Set aside to dry completely.

5. Make the foreground trees.

Cut 2 sections of trees out of cardstock (Figure F). The horizon line on these is lower than on the background trees, and the tree trunks are wider, which helps the illusion of perspective. Each tree section covers slightly less than half the width of the stage (but their bases overlap), and each has a tab on its outer edge. Fold the tabs toward the back.

Cut two ¼"-wide strips of foamcore board slightly shorter than the width of each of the foreground tree cutouts. Glue these foamcore braces to the back of the trees at the bottom, to give them more stability when they're glued to the base.

6. Mount the pieces.

Glue the cabin over the black background trees, close to their horizon line. Don't place it lower than the horizon line on the foreground trees. Tape the sides of the stage to the base so you'll be working with an upright scene for the final steps.

Glue the right piece of the foreground trees about 1" from the background trees, making room for the cabin (Figure G). They shouldn't touch each other; by leaving the small space between, you allow the foreground trees to cast shadows over the cabin.

Glue the foreground trees on the left about ½" from the front of the stage. Place the deer temporarily to measure a comfortable distance for the placement of these trees (Figure H). Make sure the deer's not too hidden behind the trees, but just peeking around them. Now glue the deer to the base of the stage.

Let everything dry and paint as desired. Then slowly slide your artwork into your frame. Enjoy!

✚ For more tips and variations, check out craftzine.com/07/design_diorama.

Patricia Zapata is a graphic designer who loves working with cut paper (alittlehut.com). She explores crafty endeavors on her blog (alittlehut.blogspot.com) and interviews inspiring artists at Crafty Synergy (craftysynergy.com).

Herbal Tinctures

Blend your own folk medicines. BY BROOKELYNN MORRIS

Herbalists are some of the original DIYers. They balk at the idea of purchasing from giant pharmaceutical companies what they can make themselves: namely, folk medicine. And they've been doing it for centuries.

It's easy and more common than you think to take herbal medicine. Munching on some parsley after dinner is one way, or sipping on chamomile tea to relieve stress is another. It's just as easy, if only a little more time-consuming, to follow ancient techniques to create your own potent tinctures that extract and preserve the qualities of many useful plants.

Photography by Nat Wilson-Heckathorn

» **Dandelions**
» **Herbal reference books**
» **Cutting board**
» **Sharp knife**
» **Blender**
» **Vodka, vegetable glycerin, or vinegar**
» **Fine mesh strainer**
» **Clean jars with airtight lids**
» **Dark glass bottles** for storage

 CLEAN GREENS

Because you'll be ingesting this tincture, the first consideration when gathering the needed herbs is location, location, location. Sure, dandelions grow in your lawn, but does your neighbor spray pesticides on them from over the fence? You might find some growing in the cracks on the edge of the street, but what about the asphalt particles and soot from cars?

Pollution does not aid digestion, so please choose only plants that are unspoiled, fresh, and pure. The plants I used in this project came from an abandoned hillside garden, an organic one at that. Bonus!

Dandelions are the perfect place to start. This common flower has many significant actions on the body. It is a bitter herb and a powerful digestive aid. Taking it in small amounts as a tonic for the body is very safe, and can be quite helpful in curing any number of ailments, including sluggish digestion and even skin breakouts. It's often seen in salads or in the ever-popular dandelion wine.

We'll be making 3 types of tinctures with dandelions: alcohol, glycerin, and vinegar. Before you start taking a tincture, I recommend, nay, insist, that you learn about the properties of herbs and the recommended dosages of tinctures. There are many excellent books and websites available on the subject. It's a wonderful way to apply the do-it-yourself spirit to your health. Check out the list of resources at craftzine.com/07/extract_herbal.

1. Gather herbs.

Find the perfect dandelion, and dig up the whole thing. The roots of dandelions are long, strong, and twisting. Do your best to get as much root matter as possible. If some of the root happens to break off, don't fret; the bit left behind will grow into a whole new plant.

At this point, hippies, witches, and shamans will thank the plant for giving up its life to create healing medicine. Although it's fringe behavior, and talking to plant spirits makes you a weirdo, can it really hurt to express gratitude to Mother Nature?

Otherwise, shake the dirt off the root ball and huck your plants into a basket: flower, seedpod, leaves, roots, and all.

2. Prep the plant matter.

In my research, I found that using the whole plant gives you the most complete tonic, but if you like, yours can be just root, just leaf, or just flower. In this example we use it all, even the spent flower heads that went to seed. The plants will be dirty. Rinse, rinse, rinse them.

After the dandelions have been cleaned, start chopping them up (Figure A, next page). Chop the roots first. The hard, dark root bark will part to reveal pure, white flesh. Juicy, milky sap will ooze out. That's the good stuff. Next, chop the leaves and stems into bits as well.

I didn't use a knife for the flower heads. Instead I waited until right before I was going to use them, then I picked them apart with my fingers. I like pulling petals off flowers — it's fun!

3. Add menstruum and blend.

Menstruum is the herbalist's word for solvent. It's the liquid in the recipe. The menstruum extracts the properties of the plant, and at the same time preserves them, almost indefinitely. I made 3 different tinctures of dandelion: 1 with alcohol, 1 with vegetable glycerin, and 1 with vinegar.

Fig. A: Finely chop all the plant matter. Fig. B: Put the dandelions in the jar and fill with menstruum to cover the plants. Fig. C: Pour it all into a blender and blend.

Fig. D: Shake the tincture every day. Fig. E: Strain the plant matter and collect the liquid. Fig. F: Store the tincture in dark bottles. Fig. G: Label your herbal medicine.

» **Alcohol** is an excellent menstruum; 100 proof grain alcohol is the best choice, but vodka, gin, or rum can be used in its place. This example uses the strongest vodka I could find at the market here in California, 80 proof (40% alcohol).

» **Vegetable glycerin** also extracts and preserves, but must be refrigerated. Glycerin is perfect for children or other people for whom alcohol is contra-indicated. It's available with a little searching. It's thick and sticky, so dilute it to 50% with spring water.

» **Vinegar** is great because it's tasty and can be used in cooking, or served on salads. I used apple cider vinegar, although white or red will also work.

Place the chopped plant matter into a jar, then pour in the menstruum until the plant matter is just barely covered with liquid (Figure B). I made 1 jar of each type of menstruum, all using the same propor-tions. Now pour the mixture into a blender. Blend to your heart's content (Figure C). I stopped when the particles of plant seemed good and pulverized, and the liquid was cloudy and milky. Pour it all back into the jar, and screw the lid on tight.

4. Wait and shake.

For the next 6 weeks, store your jar in a cool, dark place, and shake it vigorously every day (Figure D). Shaking the tincture prevents the plant matter from settling, and exposes more of its surface area to the menstruum. Shake it and then store it; store it and then shake it. Checking on the tincture every day allows you to watch the transformation from green liquid to darker brown.

5. Bottle and label.

After 6 weeks, the tincture is strong and potent. Strain the plant matter from the fluid (Figure E). Then, using a funnel, pour the tincture into a dark glass bottle for long-term storage (Figure F). Vinegar and alcohol tinctures have a very long shelf life. Glycerin tinctures do too, as long as they are refrigerated.

Oh, and don't forget to make a clear, readable label for this medicine (Figure G). Include the plant name and the parts of the plant used, the menstru-um used, and the date the tincture was made.

The natural world is Brookelynn Morris' greatest inspiration. She learned everything she knows about plants and herbs from one of her favorite teachers, her mother-in-law.

Photography by Sam Murphy

Pure Vanilla Satisfaction

Making your own excellent vanilla extract is practically effortless. BY MELISSA KRONENTHAL

Before you start jumping to all kinds of wrong conclusions about me, let me tell you what I don't do. I don't bake my own bread, roll my own pasta, or simmer my own stocks. I don't make my own yogurt, cheese, beer, wine, or jam. I don't grow my own vegetables or herbs. I don't, as a matter of course, can, pickle, bottle, or preserve much of anything. If you imagine my fridge and shelves are full of anything other than what I bought at the supermarket last time I was there, I'm sorry to say you're sorely mistaken.

I've told you all this not because I'm looking for your sympathy (or scorn), but so you can better appreciate the following. I do make my own vanilla extract, and if I can do it, I'm certain you can, too.

Materials

» **¼lb vanilla beans** or more
» **4oz (118ml) bottles of vanilla extract** (2)
» **750ml bottles of booze** (2)
   vodka, light rum, bourbon, or any mild-flavored spirit containing at least 40% alcohol
» **1qt or 1L glass container with a lid** such as a Mason jar

Yield: 1 quart or liter to begin with, and as much as you like after that

There are certainly more scientific ways to go about making vanilla extract, where you use a set ratio of beans to alcohol and let it sit exactly X number of weeks. The beauty of this method, however, is that aside from the very beginning, you're only using spent beans to make it (which feels delightfully frugal), and once you get the ball rolling, as long as you keep using vanilla beans in your kitchen, you'll have an unending supply of extract on hand, too.

Also, consider the fact that extract made this way keeps getting better and better with every bottle you produce. Pretty nifty, no?

1. Find good, cheap vanilla beans.

Many websites offer deep discounts for vanilla beans purchased in bulk, where individual beans can end up costing only pennies. I usually buy mine from San Francisco-based Vanilla Saffron Imports; other excellent sources are Patricia Rain's Vanilla Company (where you can also learn about the politics of vanilla production) and eBay.

I usually buy ½lb at a time (about 60–80 beans, depending on variety), which lasts me about a year. You'll probably have a choice between 2 varieties: Bourbon (Madagascar) beans make the deep, round extract most of us are familiar with, while Tahitian beans taste more spicy and floral. Mexican beans, harder to find, are considered by some to be the most fragrant of all. I find a mix makes the best extract.

2. Buy the vanilla extract.

You'll need two 4oz (118ml) bottles. Get something good and strong, such as Nielsen-Massey or Penzey's. Trader Joe's is fine, too. Just make sure it's real vanilla — not some nasty cocktail of chemicals — and has a flavor you'll be happy to find in your own extract. Put 1 bottle on the shelf and start using it. It's going to take a while for your homemade stuff to be ready, and you'll need something to tide you over.

The other bottle you'll be using to kick-start your homemade extract. While this step isn't strictly necessary, adding commercial extract to your own mixture will help speed the process, helping you attain a usable strength in less time than beans alone. If you don't have access to high-quality commercial extract, or if you just prefer to make your extract entirely your own, you certainly can — just be prepared for it to take a bit longer.

3. Buy two 750ml bottles of booze.

The classic base for extracts is vodka, but bourbon, light rum, or pure grain spirits also work as long as they contain at least 40% (80 proof) alcohol. Just choose something that doesn't have too strong a flavor of its own. It doesn't need to be fancy — just the standard stuff your supermarket sells.

Again, put 1 bottle in the cupboard (no, this one is not to tide you over, so hands off!). This is your "top-up" bottle, which you'll start using once you start decanting your own extract.

4. Clean your glass container.

I recommend something with a wide mouth — a Mason jar is perfect — since you'll need to reach in there and remove used beans from time to time. Clean it well. Make sure it doesn't harbor any weird odors.

5. Combine ingredients.

Pour 1 bottle of store-bought extract (Figure A) and 1 bottle of booze into your container (Figure B), then add some vanilla beans. If you've already got some used beans lying around — perhaps in a jar of sugar somewhere? — use those. If you don't, you'll have to sacrifice some new ones.

How many you start with is up to you: the more you add now, the sooner your extract will be ready. I started with 4–6 new ones, and added 3–4 used ones per month after that. If you're not supplementing your base with a bottle of commercial extract, you might want to start with double that number. Just split them lengthwise down the middle (Figure C) and throw them in (Figure D).

Fig. A: Pour a bottle of store-bought vanilla into your extraction jar as the starter. Fig. B: Add a bottle of inexpensive, not-too-strong-tasting alcohol (usually vodka). Fig. C: Split about half a dozen vanilla beans lengthwise down the middle. Fig. D: Add approximately 4–6 new beans to the starter jar. Fig. E: Add 3–4 used beans to your jar each month, or as many as you use in your day-to-day baking and cooking. The more the merrier!

6. Shake and set aside.
Put the lid on tightly and give everything a shake. Now put the container in a cool, dark cupboard.

7. Carry on with your normal life.
Make lots of cookies, cakes, custards, and ice cream. I'm sure you'll think of other uses for all that vanilla, but the important thing is that every time you use a bean, throw it in your extract container afterward. If all you've used are the seeds, simply throw in the empty pod; if you've simmered the entire bean in liquid, give it a good rinse first. Use your nose — if it still smells like vanilla, go ahead and stick it in.

8. Shake the container every week.
Feel free to poke your nose in and see how things are developing. It will start out smelling powerfully like alcohol, but over time, the vanilla flavors will take over and the boozy smell will almost disappear.

9. Do this for, oh, about 6–8 weeks.
The longer the better. What we're aiming for is that by the time you've finished that bottle of store-bought extract, your own should be rich, fragrant, and ready to start decanting.

10. Decant and top up.
When your homemade extract has reached your preferred strength, decant some into your own 4oz bottle (you can even use the handy little store bottle), or multiple little bottles, if you're going to give some away. Don't decant it all — make sure there's enough left to get your next batch started.

Now get out that second bottle of booze you stashed away all those weeks ago and top up the container so it's full again. You'll need to do this every time you decant. You can probably leave all the beans in there at this point, but if things start to get too crowded just remove a few of the mushiest ones.

Place the container back in the cupboard to mature for another couple of months and repeat Steps 7–10 as many times as you like. The extract you get from it will just keep getting better and better.

➕ Check out craftzine.com/07/extract_vanilla for resources.

Melissa Kronenthal is a food and travel writer living in Edinburgh, Scotland. When not obsessively hoarding vanilla beans, she writes the award-winning food blog travelerslunchbox.com.

Kona Kai Jewelry Stand

Build an easy-access rack for the jewels you wear most. BY MATT MARANIAN

My lovely wife has been collecting vintage jewelry for most of her adult life. Some pieces she considers "too good to wear" and keeps stashed in jewelry boxes, waiting for those special occasions that never seem to come. Others she keeps in rotation, wearing favorites often, then switching them out for other favorites. One of her longtime complaints — the lament that inspired this design — was that she wanted an easy place to park her jewels at the end of the day where she could quickly grab them the following morning, a place where she could see them, but without them getting tangled or piling up into a big mess. Since she has a weakness for low-end Hawaiiana and a love for all things aquatic, I made her a jewelry stand that's a little bit Mary Ann and a whole lotta Ginger.

Check out a how-to video at craftzine.com/07/adorn_stand

Photograph by Matt Maranian

Photography by Sam Murphy

Fig. A: Use the cam pins of the miter box to secure the bamboo while sawing. Fig. B: One end of the bamboo can be cut at an angle. Fig. C: When drilling holes for the necklace stand's arms and the bracelet stand's base, start with a smaller drill bit and widen the holes gradually to achieve a snug fit. Fig. D: Drill the indicated holes. Fig. E: The arms of the necklace stand are positioned at 3 and 7 o'clock from the stand base.

Materials

- » **Miter box**
- » **Bamboo pole** 1½" diameter, 2½' long
- » **Bamboo pole** 1" diameter, 2' long
- » **Drill and bits up to 1"**
- » **Abalone or scallop drip shell** 7" or less at its longest points
- » **5lb bag of aquarium gravel**
- » **10" plastic drip tray** The kind used underneath potted plants.
- » **Felt** the size of the dip tray
- » **16oz Castin' Craft casting resin and catalyst**
- » **Disposable container and stir stick**
- » **Sandpaper, wood glue, pencil, scissors, and Sharpie**

1. Cut the bamboo.

Using a miter box, cut the 1½" bamboo to lengths of about 20" for the necklace stand base and 9" for the bracelet stand (Figure A). Cut the 1" bamboo to 2 lengths of 6" (1 for the bracelet stand base, 1 for an arm on the necklace stand) and 1 length of 10" (for the second arm of the necklace stand). One end of the 6" and 10" lengths may be cut at a diagonal for style's sake, or all cuts may be straight, it's up to you (Figure B). Sand the edges of all the sections smooth of splinters. To keep bamboo from splintering, always sand away from the cut, never against.

2. Fit the bamboo pieces together.

Take the 20" bamboo necklace stand base and stand it upright on a table. If it doesn't stand straight, flip it and try it the other way (you might find that one of your crosscuts is straighter than the other). Once you've determined which end works better as the base, mark the base pole 2" and 6" from the top — these spots will be the levels at which the arms of the necklace stand extend.

To establish the directional positioning of the arms, imagine that the top end of the base pole is a clock face. The arms of the necklace stand will correspond to the 3 and 7 o'clock positions. Vise the bamboo securely, and drill a hole 2" from the top at the 3 o'clock spot, drilling only through 1 side of the bamboo (Figures C and D). Reposition the bamboo

Fig. F: Using a glue gun, glue the bottom rim of the stands. Fig. G: Position the stands and ring tray as you like, allowing clearance for hanging necklaces. If you're using plastic fish aquarium plants, place them now.

Fig. H: In a well-ventilated or open-air area, mix the resin in a container according to the product instructions. Fig. I: Carefully cover the gravel with resin. Fig. J: Allow the resin to set completely.

and drill another hole 6" from the top at the 7 o'clock spot, again drilling through only 1 side. Mark a spot dead center on the 9" piece, vise it securely, and drill a hole through 1 side. Sand the edges of the holes. Fit the necklace stand's arms into their holes, and the bracelet stand onto its base. Secure with wood glue, and allow to dry.

✳ **TIP: To keep the drill bit from sliding, put a piece of masking tape over the spot to be drilled.**

3. Place the stands and ring tray.

Place the plastic drip tray on a flat work surface. Position the shell (ring dish) and the necklace and bracelet stands within the drip tray at comfortable distances from one another, and mark the stand positions with a Sharpie.

Set the shell aside, and remove the stands from their spots. Run a thin ring of hot glue on the bottom edge of the necklace stand and secure it in its marked spot within the drip tray (Figure F). Repeat with the bracelet stand and other pieces you want to place (Figure G). Fill the tray with aquarium gravel to just below the brim. Push the shell into the gravel.

4. Pour the resin.

Work in a well-ventilated, dust-free area — one that you can leave for several hours while the resin is setting (seriously, this stuff is intense!). Following the instructions, mix the resin in a clean, disposable container. A 1-quart yogurt container is ideal (Figure H).

Carefully pour the resin over the gravel, being sure to coat the entire surface, and coming as close to the bamboo bases as possible without splashing them with resin (Figure I). Pour enough resin to saturate the gravel bed, stopping just short of completely submerging it. Let sit undisturbed overnight.

5. Release the base from its mold.

With a pair of sharp scissors, snip into the edge of the drip tray at spots about 5" apart around its circumference, and peel the sections of the tray away from the resin base. To keep the bottom of the stand from scratching table surfaces, glue a piece of felt to the bottom, cut about ½" smaller than the resin base.

✳ **TIP: Add extras like plastic foliage and ceiling glitter to the gravel for a tacky souvenir look.**

Matt Maranian is a best-selling author living in Brattleboro, Vt.

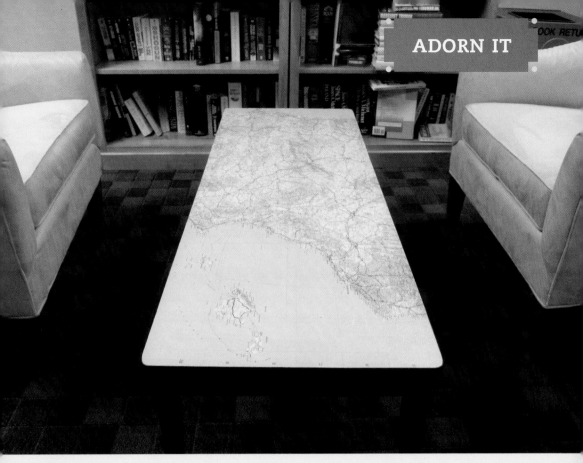

Decoupage Your World

Turn a table into a conversation piece with maps and memories from your travels. BY MARY ANDERSON

I've always loved to travel, and of all the places I've visited, Spain especially has captured my heart. What better way to keep my memories front and center (while sprucing up my living room) than by adorning my coffee table with maps of one of my favorite countries?

This project is perfect for those who love the aesthetics and romance of maps, for people who travel frequently and keep maps as souvenirs, and for those who wish they could travel more. Your new map coffee table will not only add a dash of design to your room, it'll surely inspire colorful cocktail party conversation.

Photograph by Dan Videtch

Fig. A: Paint the table. Be sure to evenly cover all sides and legs. Fig. B: Ironing the creases out of your map is a crucial step in making your table, as it will prevent bubbles from forming later in the project.

Fig. C: Creasing the map along the edges of the table will help you place it right where you want when you glue it down. Fig. D: Trim away any excess map to aid in the gluing process.

Materials

» **Coffee table**
» **Map of your choice** large enough to cover your table
» **Spray adhesive** such as Krylon
» **Mod Podge glue/sealer** for paper
» **Future floor finish** or another clear acrylic finish
» **Medium-grit sandpaper**
» **Black latex interior paint** or spray paint
» **Paintbrushes** A small roller, and large and medium craft brushes
» **Newspaper** for covering your workspace
» **Iron**
» **Scissors**
» **Hobby knife**
» **Clean rags**
» **Face mask**

1. Prep the coffee table.

Cover your workspace (under the table) with newspaper. Sand your coffee table using medium-grit sandpaper. It's not necessary to sand all the way through the finish; you just want to create a rough surface that the paint can adhere to. After you sand the table, clean it thoroughly with a damp rag and allow it to dry.

Next, paint your table (Figure A). You don't have to paint the whole tabletop (you may want to just do a border around the edges on top), but I find that painting the whole top provides a solid background for the map, should any of the table surface show through. When dry, sand the tabletop lightly so that the map will adhere well.

2. Prep the map.

Iron your map on a medium-high or high heat setting. The easiest way is to spread the map out on a carpeted floor. Make sure to iron both the front and the back thoroughly, getting the creases out as much as possible (Figure B). Once the map is flat, lay it over the top of your table and position it to your liking. Mark the edges of the table by creasing the map (Figure C). Cut the map so that it has a 2"–3" border

Photography by Cal Rebhuhn

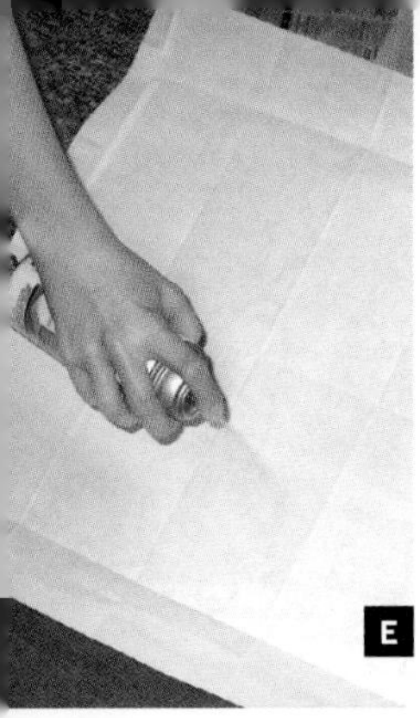

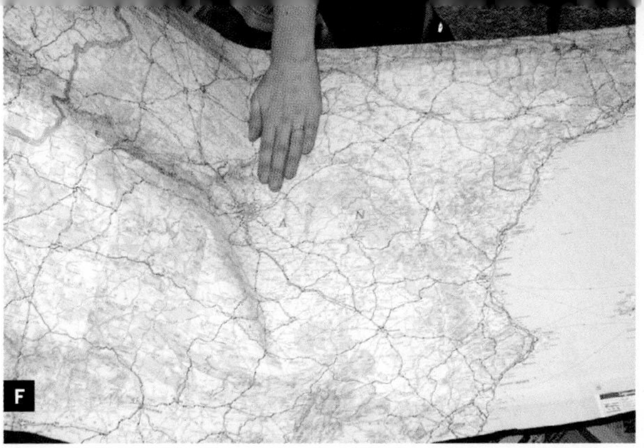

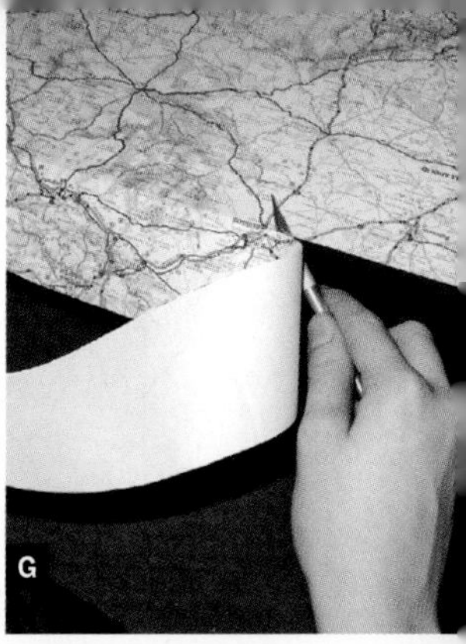

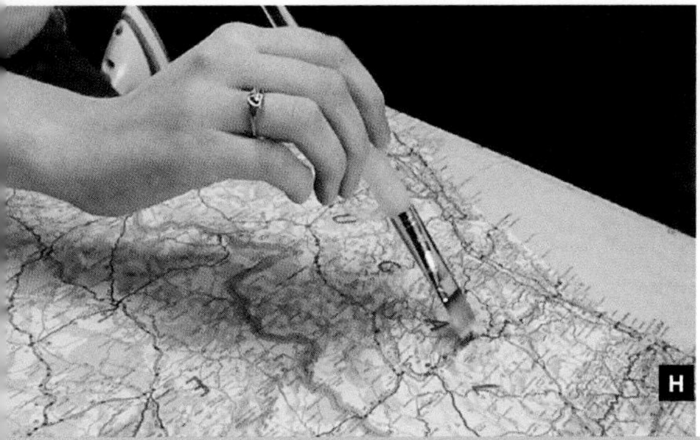

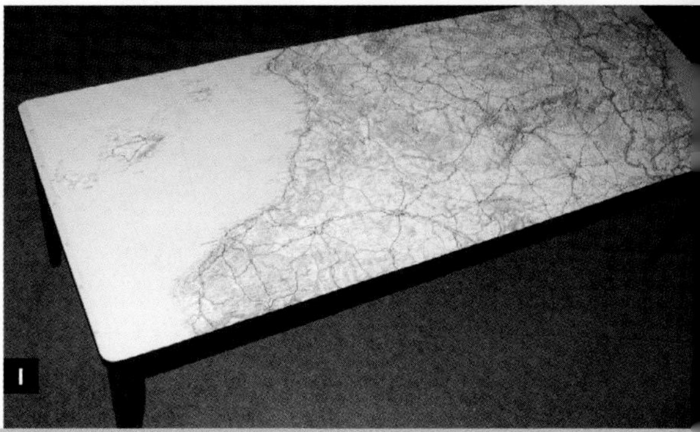

Fig. E: In a well-ventilated area, coat both the back of the map and the table with spray adhesive. Fig. F: Lay the map down on the table and smooth carefully to avoid creating bubbles. Fig. G: Carefully trim away the excess map to leave your table with clean edges. Fig. H: Cover the tabletop in a layer of Mod Podge and a few coats of acrylic finish to protect against spills and give the table a longer life. Fig. I: It's done!

around the creases you just made (Figure D). This will make working with the map much easier.

3. Mount the map.

Lay the map wrong-side up on the floor next to the table. Wearing a face mask, liberally spray both the table and the map with spray adhesive (Figure E) — use a lot more than you think you'll need. Working from one end to the other, begin placing the map onto the table (Figure F). Make sure to line up the creases you made on the map with the edges of the table. Smooth the map out very carefully as you're laying it down. Once the map is down, continue to smooth it out until it all appears to have adhered well to the table. Let the adhesive dry for about 3 hours.

TIP: If there are air bubbles after the adhesive dries, iron the table to smooth them out.

4. Finish the table.

Using scissors, make a cut from the edge of the map that leads up to 1 corner of the table. Then use your hobby knife to cut off the excess map, making the edge of the map flush with the edge of the table. An easy way to do this is to place the edge of the blade along the edge of the table, then pull the blade along, lifting the cut-off paper as you go (Figure G).

Clean off the tabletop with a dry rag. Working from one end of the table to the other, use a paintbrush to lay down a coat of Mod Podge (Figure H). If wrinkles form, many can be rubbed out with either your paintbrush or your fingers when the Mod Podge is almost dry, and most small wrinkles or bubbles will flatten out on their own as the glue continues to dry. Allow the Mod Podge to dry for at least 1 hour. It may still be tacky after it has dried, but this next step will eliminate that.

Wearing your face mask, use your paintbrush to generously coat the tabletop with Future acrylic floor finish. A little goes a long way, so you won't have to use very much. To make your table surface durable and waterproof, brush on 3 to 4 coats of the finish, allowing each coat to dry for 20 minutes. Your table will sport a wonderful glossy finish. If wrinkles appear when you're putting on the finish, don't worry; they should disappear as the table dries.

Mary Anderson is a craft-loving college student at Iowa State University and the founder of Marajane Creations (marajane01.etsy.com).

Safety Pin Jacket

Pin on some snazzy wings (or even the whole bird)
to add some sparkle to an old jacket.

BY KATHLEEN CONAHAN

Awhile ago I bought a package of 200 safety pins for a project, but only used about 50 of them. A few weeks later I looked at the pins and thought that they kind of looked like feathers. So I took a pinstripe jacket out of my closet and used the safety pins to make a pair of wings on the back. I got a lot of compliments on that jacket, so I ended up making several more. This is my most recent one.

Photography by Kathleen Conahan

» **A sturdy jacket** You're putting lots of pins into this thing, so be aware that thin fabric might tear. And fabric that's too thick is hard to work with. (I've used a few denim jackets, which work pretty well, but polyester or a wool blend is easier.) Jackets with a lining are nice, because they allow you to hide the backs of the pins by pinning through only the top layer of fabric. Also, choose fabric with a simple pattern that won't overwhelm your pin design.

» **Safety pins of various sizes** For this jacket I used sizes 0, 1, 2, and 3 steel and brass pins.

» **Pencil or light-colored chalk**

» **Needle and thread**

» **Dressmaker's dummy (optional)** The dummy lets you see the overall effect of the image as you work.

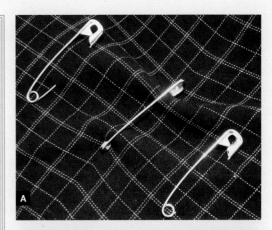

A

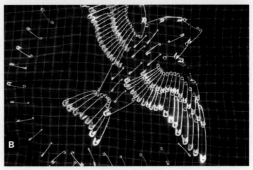

B

1. Sketch.

Choose an image for your jacket. Keep in mind that not all images translate well into this medium. Try to pick something that will take advantage of the shape and texture of the pins. When satisfied, draw your design onto the jacket with chalk or pencil.

❄ **TIP: When you close a pin, make sure you don't have too much or too little fabric inside. Too much fabric bunched up on the pin will cause the material to pucker; too little will let the pin slide out of place, possibly messing up the design. Go for a snug fit like the pin on the far right in Figure A.**

2. Start pinning.

When inserting the pins, be systematic about it. Finish an entire line before starting another; you can mess with them later if it doesn't turn out just right.

Don't be afraid to deviate a little from your original pattern. Sometimes while pinning, you realize that the design needs tweaking to make it look better.

Use different sizes and colors of pins to add variety and detail (Figure B). You can also get different effects and textures by changing the spacing of the pins. Go with the sizes that look best with your design. I end up using size 1 the most.

3. Stitch.

Gravity will tend to pull all your pins downward. If the pins need to lie a certain way, you can use a needle and thread to stitch them down (I use silver thread because it's less visible.) This will stop them from moving around when you wear the jacket, but it's not always necessary.

4. Wear and enjoy!

Go and show off your awesome new bit of wearable art! These jackets are extremely versatile, great for formal or casual occasions. They're machine washable; run them on delicate and line-dry them right away. Don't put them through the dryer, though — that could end painfully with scorched fingers.

Kathleen Conahan is a clothes hacker living in Portland, Ore. If you ever need a safety pin (or ten), she'd be the one to ask.

Simply Socks

Learn to knit a pair of comfy socks that fit.

BY MEREDITH DAVEY

I've always loved knitting. My mother first taught me when I was a child, and I've been at it ever since. But I didn't pick up socks until graduate school. In retrospect, this surprises me — they're so much fun! They're knit in the round (hardly any purling), they're wonderfully portable, and they're small, so they finish up really fast. Now, I'm always working on at least one pair.

If you're a knitter who's never tried socks before, now is your chance! This pattern gives you a basic cuff-down sock for a woman with a size 8 foot.

Photography by Andrea Dunlap (this page) and Meredith Davey (opposite page)

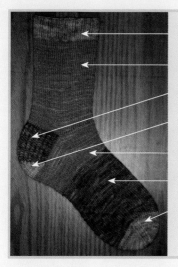

Cuff

Leg

Heel flap

Heel turn

Gusset

Foot

Toe

Socks basically consist of 7 knitted sections: the cuff, leg, heel flap, heel turn, gusset, foot, and toe (above). For the sock above, I knit different parts of the sock in different colors.However, remember that when you knit your sock, it's easiest to use one color. The different colors are for demonstration purposes, however lovely they may be. The yarn used for the step-by-step photos is a variegated yarn, which looks more complicated than it is.

1. Find your stitch gauge.
Cast on 30 stitches and knit a swatch at least 2" long. Cast off. You should have 16 stitches/2". If there are too few stitches, knit another swatch with smaller needles; if too many, knit another with larger needles. The correct gauge is very important for a proper fit.

2. Cast on.
Cast on 64 stitches over two DPN, using the same cast-on you used for your gauge. (I like the long-tail cast-on.)

3. Knit the cuff (green).
Distribute your stitches evenly over 4 needles (16 stitches each). Forming the needles into a circle, join the stitches in the round, being careful not to twist the stitches. Attach your detachable stitch marker at the beginning of your row. Move this marker along vertically as you work. Repeat the following pattern: *k2, p2*, until you reach the end of the row. Continue this 2×2 ribbing for 1½". The completed

SIZE MY SOCKS

OK, so obviously we all don't have size 8 feet. If your feet are a different size, here's how to modify the sock pattern so it will fit you.

» Measure the widest part around your foot in inches. Divide 128 by this number. This is the number of stitches per 2" in your gauge.

» Using an appropriate size of DPN (smaller for smaller feet, larger for larger feet) and your new gauge, follow the stitch gauge instructions in Step 1.

HINT: Be conservative. You'll probably only need to change your DPN from size 1 by one or two sizes. Also, most local yarn stores are very good about letting you return needles that are the wrong size.

» Follow the pattern as normal until you get to knitting the foot. Here, instead of knitting the foot until it measures 7½" from the heel, knit until it measures 2" less than the length of your own foot. Then finish the pattern as normal.

cuff is shown in Figure A, next page.

4. Knit the leg (pink).
Knit evenly for 5" (6½" total), remembering to move the detachable stitch marker along vertically as you knit each row.

5. Knit the heel flap (blue).
Remove the stitch marker and set it aside. K32 stitches onto 1 needle. Put the remaining 32 stitches on the stitch holder. Then sl1, p31 back along the needle (Figure B).

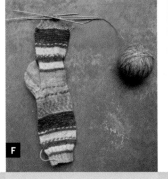

Fig. A: The finished cuff. Fig. B: The stitches split between the stitch holder and 1 needle, with the completed heel flap. Fig. C: The heel after it's been turned. Fig. D: After you've picked up and knit the stitches along the heel flap edges, rearrange the stitches on 4 needles. Fig. E: The finished gusset. Fig. F: The almost completed sock. Fig. G: Put the last 16 stitches on 2 needles.

The rest of the heel is knit in a style called the "Eye of the Partridge," which is worked as follows:

» **Row 1 (RS):** *sl1, k1*.
» **Row 2 (WS):** sl1, purl to the end.

Repeat rows 1 and 2, 15 times, for 30 rows total, ending with a WS. The completed heel flap is shown in Figure C.

6. Turn the heel (green).

On the next RS row, k19, ssk, k1, then turn your knitting so you are prepared to work the WS (despite being in the middle of the row!). Over the next 11 rows, work your heel as follows:

```
sl1, p7, p2tog, p1, turn.
sl1, k8, ssk, k1, turn.
sl1, p9, p2tog, p1, turn.
sl1, k10, ssk, k1, turn.
sl1, p11, p2tog, p1, turn.
sl1, k12, ssk, k1, turn.
sl1, p13, p2tog, p1, turn.
sl1, k14, ssk, k1, turn.
sl1, p15, p2tog, p1, turn.
sl1, k16, ssk, k1, turn.
sl1, p17, p2tog, p1, turn.
```

You should have 20 stitches across, and your completed turned heel should look like Figure C (your yarn may be on the other side).

7. Knit the gusset (pink).

If necessary, K20 across the heel. On needle 2, pick up 18 stitches from the edge of the heel flap and knit them through the back of the stitch. Pick up a 19th "corner stitch" where the heel flap meets the stitch-holder (Figure E). Twist and knit this stitch, so a hole doesn't form.

Slip the stitches from the stitch holder onto needle 3 and knit them. Use needle 4 to pick up, twist, and knit the next "corner stitch," followed by 18 stitches along the other heel flap edge. Continue knitting 10 stitches from needle 1, giving you 29 stitches on needle 4. This causes a break between needles at the heel center. Place your detachable stitch marker there. This is now the beginning of your row.

You have no doubt noticed that you have many more stitches than you started with. You will decrease these extra stitches out in gussets. First, however, you need to rearrange your stitches (starting from the center of the heel), so the needles have the following numbers:

Photography by Arwen O'Reilly (this page) and Andrea Dunlap (opposite page)

Needle 1: 29 stitches
Needles 2 & 3: 16 stitches
Needle 4: 29 stitches

To create the gussets, knit the next 2 rows as follows:

» **Row 1:**

Needle 1: K to last 2 stitches, k2tog.
Needles 2 & 3: K.
Needle 4: ssk, knit to end of row.

» **Row 2:** K entire row.

Repeat rows 1 and 2, 13 times, until only 16 stitches are left on needles 1 and 4 (64 stitches total). The finished gusset is shown in Figure E.

8. Knit the foot (blue).

After finishing the gusset, knit evenly until the sock measures 7½" from the end of the heel, or 2" less than the length of your foot.

9. Knit the toe (green).

K16, and shift your detachable marker from between needles 4 and 1 to between needles 1 and 2. Your row now begins with needle 2.

To create the toe, knit the following 2 rounds:

» **Row 1:**

Needles 2 & 4: k1, ssk, knit to end.
Needles 3 & 1: K to last 3 stitches, k2tog, k1.

» **Row 2:** Knit.

Repeat rows 1 and 2 until 32 stitches remain. Then, repeat row 1 until 16 stitches remain. Put the final 16 stitches on 2 needles (Figure G), grouping stitches from needles 2 and 3 together (the top of the foot) and needles 4 and 1 together (the bottom of the foot).

Cut your yarn, leaving a 12" tail, and thread it onto the blunt tapestry needle. Graft the toe with the 12" tail by doing the Kitchener stitch through the remaining stitches (described in the box on the right).

10. Finish.

Using the tapestry needle, weave in any loose ends.

➕ For a list of knitting abbreviations used here, go to craftzine.com/07/wear_socks.

Meredith Davey is a Ph.D. astrophysicist who would much rather be knitting. She splits her time between her research in Boulder, Colo., and her husband and cats in Boston, Mass.

THE KITCHENER STITCH

1. Pass the tapestry needle through the first stitch on the front knitting needle as if to knit. Drop that stitch off the needle and pull the yarn through.

2. Slide the needle through the next stitch on the front knitting needle as if to purl. Leave this stitch on the needle.

3. Pass the needle through the first stitch on the back knitting needle as if to purl. Drop that stitch off the needle and pull the yarn through.

4. Slide the needle through the next stitch on the back knitting needle as if to knit. Leave this stitch on the needle.

5. Repeat Steps 1–4 until all stitches are grafted together.

Granny Gets Wired
Crochet a granny square that sparkles.

BY DIANE GILLELAND

Crocheted in fine-gauge wire, the humble granny square becomes something shiny and elegant. If you're already familiar with yarn crochet, give wire a whirl. With a little practice, you'll be turning out lovely metallic granny squares.

You can use them to make jewelry or appliqués for handbags or hats. Or make a large granny square, add a fabric backing, and you have the basis for a cool zippered pouch. The possibilities are endless!

Photography by Diane Gilleland

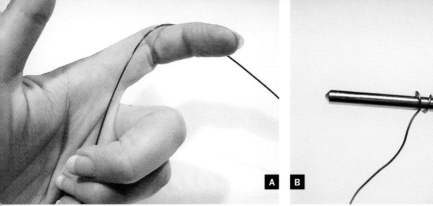

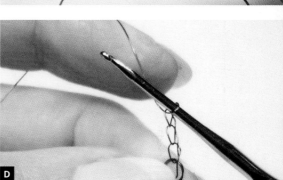

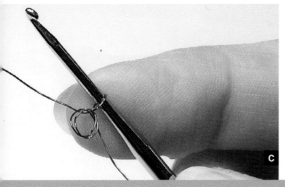

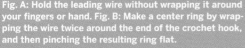

Fig. A: Hold the leading wire without wrapping it around your fingers or hand. Fig. B: Make a center ring by wrapping the wire twice around the end of the crochet hook, and then pinching the resulting ring flat.

Fig. C: Put your hook through the ring, and draw a loop of wire back through it. This loop is the basis for your initial chain stitches. Fig. D: Chain 3 stitches to begin the granny square.

Materials

» **30-gauge coated copper craft wire in assorted colors** available from Fire Mountain Gems, firemountaingems.com
» **Steel crochet hook, U.S. size 6**
» **Wire cutters**

NOTE: Gauge is not important for this project. If a U.S. size 6 hook feels too small for you, try a larger one. Note that with a larger hook, your resulting granny square will have a lacier appearance.

» This article assumes you have some basic crochet skills. If you've never crocheted a granny square in yarn before, we recommend practicing a few times before you try it with wire.

❄ TIPS

Take care of your hands. Wire is much stiffer than yarn, and requires the muscles in your hands to work harder. When you crochet with wire, it's important to take breaks every now and then to stretch and relax. And although it may be terribly compelling, I don't recommend wire crocheting for hours at a time — you can end up with really sore hands the next day.

Wire can break. Be very careful not to let your wire develop kinks as you work. With wire this fine, any point where it kinks is a point where it can easily break. And you don't want it breaking in mid-stitch!

Wire won't frog. One of the great joys of yarn crochet is that if your work isn't turning out the way you'd like, you can always pull the stitches out and start again. Not so with wire. The crochet process creates too many kinks in the wire, so it can't be reused. If you make a mistake, cut the wire and start fresh.

How to hold your wire. Many crocheters wrap the leading strand of their yarn around their hand or fingers to help maintain tension. When you crochet with wire, you'll want to adopt a much simpler hold, as in Figure A. The stiffness of the wire pretty much creates its own tension, and wrapping the wire around your fingers could cut off circulation.

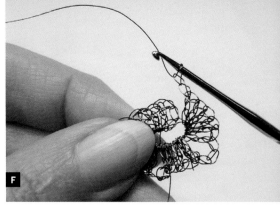

Fig. E: Gently pinch each cluster of 6 double crochets together. Fig. F: At the end of the first row, slip-stitch across to the start of the second row. Fig. G: At the end of each row, insert your hook into the chain-2 spaces at the corners, and pull them gently outward. Fig. H: "Block" the first row by shaping your work into a square with your fingers. Weave in loose ends and cut them close to your work.

1. Make a central ring.

In yarn crochet, you make a central ring by chaining a few stitches and joining them together. But with wire crochet, you'll want a smoother ring. Instead of chaining, just wrap the wire around the hook twice, as in Figure B, and pinch the resulting ring flat.

2. Pull up a loop.

Hold the ring as shown in Figure C, then put your hook through the ring, yarn over (or in this case, wire over), and pull a loop back through the ring. This loop becomes the foundation of your initial chains.

3. Begin your double crochets.

From this point, you can follow the crochet diagram provided on the next page. This text will provide you with some key tips along the way.

Or, if you don't like crochet diagrams, use your favorite classic granny square pattern, with this adjustment: when you make a granny square in yarn, you usually need only 3 double crochets to make each cluster. Because wire is so much thinner than yarn, you'll need to make 6 double crochets per cluster.

4. Groom as you work.

After you complete each cluster, take a moment to pinch it gently together, as in Figure E. When you stop crocheting to groom the piece, pull the loop of wire on the hook out a bit, so you don't lose it. As thin as the wire is, it helps to give it a little shaping as you work. Do this as you finish crocheting each cluster. Any time you stop crocheting to groom your work, gently pull on the loop around your hook, so it enlarges. Then you can set your hook down without losing your place. When you're ready to continue crocheting, just pull the leading wire to retighten this loop around your hook.

5. Complete a row.

When making a granny square in yarn, you usually finish each row by slip-stitching your way to the starting position for the next row. The same thing applies in wire, but you may find it harder to see the places to insert your hook for the slip stitches. Luckily, wire is pretty forgiving. If you can't see the correct locations, just insert your hook into any loop that's in the vicinity of where you need to be, and complete your slip stitch. It won't be noticeable.

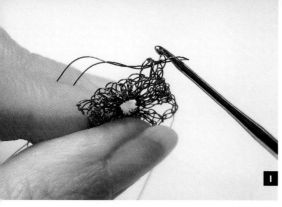

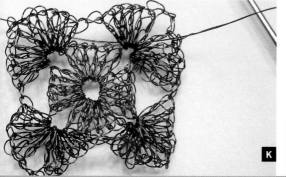

Fig. I: Add a new color by slip-stitching through the chain-2 space at the corner. Fig. J: Once you've crocheted 1 corner of the new row, take a moment to weave in and cut off any loose ends.

Fig. K: Row 2 before blocking. Fig. L: Row 2 after blocking. Fig. M: At the end of the last row, make a slip stitch with the end of the wire. Weave in the end and cut it off close to your work.

6. "Block" the first row.

Before you begin the next row, take a moment and "block" the first one. Use the end of your hook to pull the corners out to neat points, as in Figure G. And mash the corners flat — this makes it easier for the next row of stitches to slide along them. While you're at it, gently pull and stretch your work into a flat, square shape. And as a last step, weave in the loose end of the wire, and cut it off close to your work, as in Figure H.

7. Add another color.

If you want to change colors, do it the same way you'd do it with yarn — with a slip stitch. For extra stability, I insert my hook through the chain-2 space at the corner and slip-stitch through that, as in Figure I.

Once I've completed the first corner of the new row, I always stop a moment and weave in my loose ends (Figure J). Loose ends can really get in your way … and poke you.

Add as many rows to your granny square, in as many colors, as you'd like. Be sure to block your work at the end of each row (Figure L), as you did in Step 6.

8. Finish your granny square.

When you've completed your last row, slip-stitch the end of the wire, as in Figure M. Cut it close to your work. Block that last row.

9. Flatten it out.

If you want to flatten your granny square out a bit, you can place it under a stack of heavy books overnight.

Diane Gilleland produces CraftyPod (craftypod.com), a blog and podcast about making stuff.

Pulsating Pal

A vibrating pillow is just what every room needs.

BY ANNIE SHAO AND RACHEL McCONNELL

T here are pillows that look good, and there are pillows that feel good. For those inclined to add a little buzz to their home décor, try making this fun vib-illow. Take an arcade push button, a couple of batteries, and a cellphone vibrator and you've got a super simple circuit that anyone can make. Then push the button to discover the pillow's secret surprise.

If you've never soldered, don't fret. We've got a soldering tutorial for you at craftzine.com/go/solder.

Photography by Sam Murphy (this page) and Ed Troxell

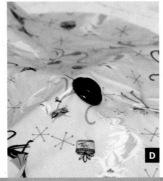
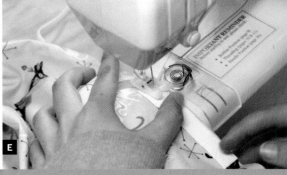

Fig. A: For your first pillow, start with an easy shape, like a heart or circle. Fig. B: Arcade push buttons tend to be large, which makes the motor easier to turn on and off.

Figs. C–D: Attach the button to the fabric from the front, then screw the nut on from the back. Fig. E: Sew velcro to corresponding spots on the front and back of the pillow.

Materials

- » **Battery holder and batteries (2 AA)**
- » **Plastic spoon**
- » **Pager or cellphone vibrator motor**
- » **Arcade push button switch** easily found on eBay
- » **Fabric** for pillow cover
- » **Interfacing fabric** thicker than cover fabric
- » **Velcro, thread, and stuffing**
- » **Insulated wire**
- » **Solder and soldering iron**
- » **Electrical tape**
- » **Hot glue gun**
- » **Sewing equipment** either machine or hand

1. Make the pillow.

Draw a pattern for your pillow on paper. Start with a simple shape, such as a circle or a heart. This line is your *sew line*. Add ⅝" around every edge to allow

yourself room for sewing. This new line is your *cut line*. Cut out the paper pattern following the cut line.

Transfer both the sew line and the cut line from the paper pattern onto the back of the fabric. (If you'd like to use fur, we advise using it only for the front of the pillow to reduce bulk and make it easier to sew and reduce bulk.) Do this twice, so you have 2 pieces of fabric, 1 for the front of your pillow and 1 for the back. If your pattern isn't symmetrical, cut the back piece with the pattern reversed so that the front of the backing fabric is on the outside of the pillow.

Cut out your fabric following the cut line (Figure A). If cutting fur, it's easier to cut the back of the fabric by sliding your scissors under the backing of the fur fabric instead of cutting the fur pile.

2. Assemble the button switch.

Disassemble the arcade button and switch assembly. You should have 3 parts: the plastic pressable button with screw threads, the matching plastic nut, and the actual microswitch (aka "cherry switch") with leads that can be soldered (Figure B).

Mark on the back of the fabric where you want the button to go, then cut out a hole slightly

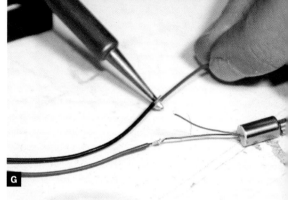

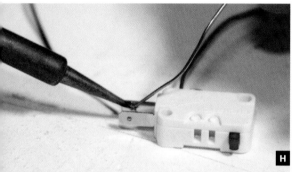

Fig. F: Sew the fronts of the fabrics facing each other along the sew line. Fig. G: Don't be intimidated if you've never soldered before — it's easy once you get the hang of it. Solder 1 wire from the battery holder to 1 lead of the vibrating motor. Fig. H: It doesn't matter which wire goes to which lead when you're soldering the wires to 2 cherry switch leads. Fig. I: Be careful not to glue the rotating part of the battery holder.

smaller than the actual button, so the fit is tight. Cut a piece of interfacing that's a couple of inches larger than the hole in the fabric, then cut a hole in the interfacing the same size as the hole in the fabric. The interfacing adds extra bulk and stiffness for the button nut to grab onto, so it won't fall out when pressed. If your interfacing is the iron-on type, iron it onto the back of the fabric, matching up the holes. If it's not iron-on, just pin it together while you attach the button.

Attach the button to the fabric. Place it through the fabric and interfacing from the front, then screw the nut on from the back, so the button is held in place as if the fabric were the arcade cabinet the button originally came from (Figures C and D).

3. Attach the velcro.

Cut 2 pieces of velcro 4"–6" long, one of the hook side and one of the loop side. Sew one to the front of the pillow (right side), along the edge, between the cut line and the sew line. Sew the other to the matching area on the back of the pillow (Figure E).

4. Put the pillow together.

Place the front and back pieces of the pillow together, with the fronts of the fabric (right sides) facing each other (as shown in Figure F). Starting at one edge of the velcro pieces, sew all the way around along the sew line. Make sure not to sew over the top of the velcro or you won't be able to turn the pillow right-side out!

5. Solder the wires.

Remember to never solder with anything in the "on" position. Take 1 wire from the battery holder, and solder it to 1 lead of the vibrator motor (Figure G). It doesn't matter which battery wire goes to the motor — positive will make it spin one way, and negative will make it spin the other way, but it still vibrates the same. Then cut a piece of insulated wire 3"–4" long and strip the ends. Solder 1 end to the remaining lead of the motor. Tape these connections to prevent short circuits.

Next, you must determine which of the cherry switch leads to solder to. If your switch has only 2 leads, those are the right ones. But if your switch has 3 leads, you need to test to see which 2 to use. Put batteries in the battery holder and hold the switch in the "on" position (you may need to tape it or get someone to help you). Hold the wire from

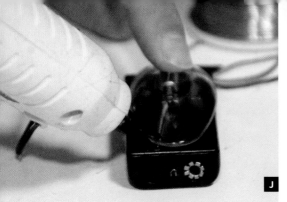

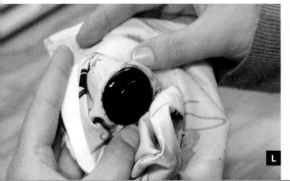

Fig. J: You can use parts of a plastic milk jug or anything else that fits to cover the motor, but we used a plastic spoon. **Fig. K:** The button assembly reattaches to the cherry switch. **Fig. L:** It's time to flip the fabric right-side out through the hole where you sewed the velcro. **Fig. M:** Press the button and feel the buzz!

Photography by Ed Troxell (J–M) and Annie Shao (bottom images)

the battery holder in one hand and the wire from the other lead of the motor in the other, and touch 2 switch leads at a time, in turn. One set of 2 leads will cause the motor to vibrate. Mark that set and remove the batteries.

Solder the wires to your 2 cherry switch leads (Figure H). It doesn't matter which wire goes to which lead here either. Test your motor again to make sure the circuit is working.

6. Attach and cover the motor.

Hot-glue the motor body onto the back of the battery holder, making sure not to glue the part that rotates (Figure I). To prevent the stuffing from catching in the motor, you need to cover the motor. We used the top of a plastic spoon, hot-glued on (Figure J), but you can use parts of a plastic milk jug or anything that fits. Make sure there's enough room for the motor to rotate all the way around.

7. Assemble all the pieces.

Reattach the cherry switch to the button assembly (Figure K). Turn the fabric right-side out through the hole where you sewed the velcro (Figure L). Then stuff the pillow, close the velcro, and play (Figure M)!

You can make all kinds of vib-illows!

📷 Check out more of the authors' projects at craftzine.com/08/wire_pillow.

Rachel McConnell was once a professional seamstress and is now a professional computer programmer. Annie Shao was once a professional computer programmer and now runs HungryPandA Clothing as a professional seamstress.

101:

UPHOLSTERY

By Ashley Jameson Eriksmoen

Add comfort and a fresh new look to your chairs.

Dining chairs are an integral part of good times. Where there's dinner, wine, and company, there are chairs. But old dining chairs are notoriously uncomfortable: no fun for the buns. With simple modifications, though, that can be remedied. Plywood slip seats can be altered to allow for a bit of flex, a tad of padding, and a big difference in comfort. At your next dinner party, don't be surprised if your guests won't leave!

This article teaches you the basics of upholstery, and our online supplement at craftzine.com/07/101 includes additional techniques for softening that slip seat. After this project, you'll be ready to graduate to reupholstering an armchair or a chair with a loose cushion.

»

BASICS »

Upholstering with tacks is the most traditional method, and the least expensive for startup costs. You just need an upholsterer's brass tack hammer with a magnetic tip and tacks. Any stapling described in this article can be accomplished with tacks. Or you can use a pneumatic upholstery staple gun, which is fast, easy on the wrists, and gentle on the fabric.

Not all fabrics are appropriate to use for upholstery. Upholstery fabric should be a weave, never a knit, and should have very little stretch along the grain. It should be sturdy enough to withstand having staples put in and ripped out. Jacquards, brocades, denims, and heavyweight woven wools are all good choices.

A slip seat is a removable upholstered seat that fits into an open chair frame.

START »

1. PREPARE YOUR CHAIR

1a. Check the frame and remove the seat. You want to start with a chair frame that's in good repair (Figure A). Check for loose joints and for cracks in the wood. See if the chair is structurally sound by giving it a good wiggle. Turn the chair upside down into a secure position. Remove only the screws that go straight down to fasten the seat to the frame; leave the horizontal screws on the cross-bracing (Figure B). Remove the seat, and put the screws in a safe place where you can actually find them later.

1b. Rip and strip. Time to put on your safety glasses: tacks and staples make unpredictable trajectories when you yank on them. If you can't get ahold of a proper staple remover, an oyster shucker will do the trick. You'll need to remove all the staples and/or tacks from the seat before you reupholster (Figure C). This is a tedious chore, but necessary so that the new staples can penetrate the wood.

1c. Check the seat. If the plywood seat pan looks cracked or weak, get a fresh piece of high-grade Europly. The thickness of your seat pan will help to determine whether to make a webbed seat or a slotted seat. (Instructions for these techniques are available at craftzine.com/07/101.)

MATERIALS

» DINING CHAIR WITH SLIP SEAT
» MANUAL SCREWDRIVER
» SAFETY GLASSES
» STAPLE REMOVER OR OYSTER SHUCKER
» TACK REMOVER OR RIPPING CHISEL
» NEEDLENOSE PLIERS
» HAMMER AND SCISSORS
» PENCIL AND RULER
» UPHOLSTERER'S TACK HAMMER AND BOX OF 4OZ BLUE STERILIZED UPHOLSTERER'S TACKS, OR STAPLE GUN AND 9/16" OR 5/8" STAPLES
» SPRAY ADHESIVE SUCH AS 3M SUPER 77 OR A SPECIAL FOAM ADHESIVE, LIKE 3M FOAMFAST 74 ADHESIVE
» HR 30 POLYURETHANE FOAM, 24"×48"×1" THICK, OR SIMILAR DENSITY NATURAL LATEX
» POLYESTER BATTING OR COTTON WADDING, 2/3YD
» FABRIC, 2/3YD, FOR SEAT COVERING

A

B

C

2. PAD THE SEAT

2a. Trace your seat onto the foam (Figure D). Mark another outline ½" beyond the edge of the seat. With the foam on a flat surface, cut along the outer lines. I use an electric turkey slicer that cuts very clean lines in foam, but if it's 1" thick or less, sharp scissors work. Cut perpendicularly so the edge of your foam is squared, not beveled. If 1" of foam isn't enough, repeat to make a second layer.

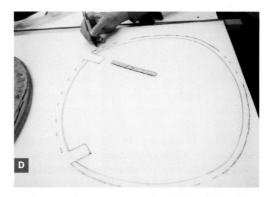

2b. Take the seat pan, foam, and spray adhesive to a well-ventilated area. Use spray adhesive to coat the surfaces of the seat pan and the foam. Once it's tacky, flip the seat onto the foam, which should extend ½" beyond the seat (Figure E). Put an over-sized piece of batting on a flat surface. With your seat foam-side down, center it on top of the batting. Gently lift the batting up to the bottom of the seat, and trim the batting to cover the bottom seat edge, approximately 2" oversized all around.

3. COVER THE SEAT WITH FABRIC

3a. Fold the fabric in half lengthwise and mark the midpoints of the edges with chalk, or notch them with scissors. Do the same folding the fabric across its width. On the underside of the seat pan, measure and mark the center of the sides, front, and back (Figure F). Place the fabric on the table right-side down, and center the oversized batting and upside-down seat on top of it. Line up the center marks in the fabric with the center marks on the seat. This is critical if your fabric has stripes or linear patterns.

3b. Gently pull the batting and fabric up around the front edge of the seat pan. Shoot 1 staple or hammer 1 tack to secure the center point of the fabric about ½" to 1" inside the seat edge (Figure G). Keeping everything aligned, stretch the fabric across the seat and secure with 1 staple to the center of the back. Pull firmly enough to soften the cut edges of the foam, to create a slight dome, and to ensure there's no slack in the seat, but don't overstretch the fabric and cause ripples or divots along the edge. Repeat this at the centers of the sides.

3c. Flip the seat right-side up and take a look. If your fabric is misaligned, you'll need to pull the staples or tacks and try again. One trick is to put in easy-to-pull "temporary" tacks or staples while you're placing your fabric. Do this by hammering in your tack only halfway, or by rolling the tip of your staple gun onto one corner, so the staple goes in at a 45° angle, leaving a triangular opening.

3d. If you have a round seat, divide the space between your center point staples, pull the fabric into place, and staple (Figure H). Split the difference again so that the fabric is evenly distributed around the rim and secured in about 16 spots. Pull and staple the remaining areas to keep the fabric taut and even all the way around (Figure I). Trim the excess fabric about ½" from the staples (Figure J). If you have a rectangular seat, work your way from the centers toward the corners, pulling the fabric taut as you go. Place staples in a row no more than ¼" apart to create an even edge. Stop about 2" short of the corners.

3e. Remove any extra bunched-up batting from the corner area (Figure K). Pull the fabric diagonally

across the corner point, and place 1 staple about 1" in from the edge. On both sides of the corner, turn the remaining fabric at the corner back under itself to form a triangular pleat. Pull that straight over the edge, and finish stapling the fabric down. Trim the excess fabric about ½" in from the staples.

3f. Unless you have notches or welting to complete, you're almost done. If there are any notches cut into the seat pan (Figure L) to let in the legs, you have some tricky cuts to make. Flip the seat upside down again. Cut the fabric down the center of the notch, stopping about 1" short of the bottom of the notch. Continue the cut in a Y shape, heading toward the 2 corners of the notch, stopping about ½" short of the actual corners (Figure M). If you cut too deep, it can show on the chair seat. Yank the triangle of the Y down as tight as you can, and pop a staple into that piece, staying as far from the edge of the fabric as possible so that it won't fray (Figure N). You won't have much room to work, so do the best you can.

Once the triangle piece is secure, yank down the flaps on the sides of the notch and staple them to

the walls of the notch (Figure N). If a rectangular seat has square notches at the corners, instead of cutting a Y, cut a 45° diagonal line toward the corner, again stopping at least ½" short of the actual corner.

3g. Your seat is done. Pop it back onto the chair frame, and screw it back into place (Figure O). Then take a load off. You deserve it!

FINISH ☒

Ashley Jameson Eriksmoen teaches upholstery, woodworking, and furniture design at City College of San Francisco, California College of the Arts, College of the Redwoods, and craft centers including Penland School of Crafts in North Carolina and Anderson Ranch Arts Center in Colorado. She designs and builds sculpture and furniture at her studio in Oakland, Calif., and exhibits nationally. ashleyeriksmoen.com

LEARN MORE:

WEBBING: Rough jute upholstery webbing woven in a simple over-and-under pattern will add a lot of give to the seat, making it much more comfortable to sit on.

SLOTTING: Sometimes the seat is ½" thick or less, and won't hold up to webbing. You can still give it greater spring by incising slots into the seat.

WELTING: This is a roll of matching or contrasting fabric that can hide staples or glue, or can be added to the edge of a slip seat for visual interest.

➕ 📷 These techniques are described in detail at craftzine.com/07/101.

READY, AIM, SHOOT!

Build a real bow and arrow to practice
your shooting skills.

By Kathreen Ricketson, Rob Shugg, and Orlando Shugg

Bow:
» Bamboo pole
» Jute twine
» Nylon string
» Epoxy glue
» Sander
» Trimming knife
» Hacksaw
» Fine-tooth hacksaw blades (2)
» Axe
» Clamp
» Scissors
» Safety gloves

Arrow:
» ¼" dowel
» Feathers
» Cotton string
» Binding varnish or nail polish
» Hacksaw
» Tape measure
» Pencil sharpener

Target:
» Cardboard
» Paint
» Brushes

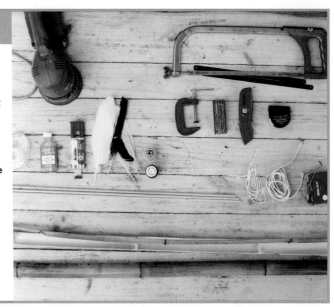

A s a boy, my partner Rob Shugg always had a bow and arrow. He was quite a little ragamuffin and had a wonderfully free and adventurous childhood, very different from all the cautionary parenting of today.

With the resurgence of books about adventures for kids and 19th-century DIY projects, some of these more exciting pastimes are enjoying a comeback. Rob wanted to share some of these adventures with our son, 5-year-old Orlando, who is only too happy to go along for the ride. Making the bow and arrow is their first step toward a bush camping trip they're planning for later in the year.

For this father-and-son weekend project, we made a simple, safe, and sturdy bundle bow out of bamboo that's fairly quick to make with materials available at any hardware shop. We chose bamboo because of its strength, flexibility, and availability, but other

⚠ CAUTION: **Though kids will love playing with a bow and arrow, please remember that it can be a dangerous weapon if not used correctly.**

materials, such as straight sticks or fiberglass, can be used.

A bundle bow, also called a quick bow, is made from a few straight sticks of varying length that are bound into a bundle. Bundling sticks of different lengths adds stiffness to the center of the bow and allows flexibility toward the limbs.

The trick to getting the bow to bend correctly is to make it symmetrical, with tension that gradually tapers off toward the ends. The shortest stick is half the length of the longest one, while the middle sticks extend somewhere in between.

Kathreen Ricketson is an artist, designer, and mother based in Australia. She is the editor of the online multi-author craft website whipup.net and runs a community photography project called selfportraitchallenge.net.

1. MAKE THE BOW

A. SHAPE THE BOW'S CENTER

Using a small axe, split the bamboo into 1"-wide strips (Figure A). You'll need 4 straight, cut, and trimmed sticks in total. From the ground, measure the length of the bamboo against the intended user, mark the spot at the user's forehead, then cut 1 piece of bamboo to that length, 1 to half that length, and 2 lengths in between (Figure B). When the 4 are clumped together, the center should be about 1" square.

B. SMOOTH OUT THE STICKS

Trim the bamboo sticks with the trimming knife, then sand them down with the sander (Figure C). Make them all as even in thickness and width as you can.

Also sand the internal knobs of the bamboo to make it smooth all over. Sand and whittle a little until the pieces lay flat against each other. Bamboo edges can be sharp, so you may want to wear safety gloves.

C. NOTCH THE ENDS

Use the trimming knife to make the notch at each end of the longest bamboo stick (Figure D) for the string to sit on. By cutting just outside the bamboo knot at each end, you'll minimize splitting later.

D. TIE THE STICKS TOGETHER

Starting with the 2 longest sticks, lash together each piece of bamboo firmly as you go, using strong twine such as jute, hemp, or linen (Figure E). Knot firmly using a whip finish knot. Test the symmetry of the bend by flexing the bundled lengths.

E. MAKE THE ARROW REST AND HANDLE

Wrap a stiff, thick nylon cord around the center section of the bow and use a hidden whip finish knot to make a smooth finish (Figures F and G). This does double duty as the arrow rest and the handle; make it slightly bigger than the user's hand.

F. MAKE THE BOWSTRING

Use a nylon or polyester cord to make the bowstring (thin enough to fit the small arrow you'll make, but not so thin that it will cut small fingers). Tie one end of the string with a hitch knot, then the other end with a loop formed by a bowline or figure-eight loop. Use trial and error to get the length just right.

G. STRING THE BOW

Fasten the hitch knot over 1 notch and place that end of the bow on the ground. Hold the other end up and bend the bow to slip the loop over the top notch. It's best to unstring the bow when it's not in use.

2. MAKE THE ARROW

A. CUT THE DOWEL

To measure the correct length of the arrow for the user, ask her or him to draw the bow using an extra-long piece of dowel, and mark the shaft 1" in front of the spot where the dowel touches the arrow rest. Cut the lengths of dowel (look for those that have a straight grain running parallel with the shaft).

B. CUT THE NOCK AND SHARPEN

The nock keeps the arrow in place on the string when the bow is drawn. To your hacksaw, attach 2 fine blades together in opposite directions. Clamp the dowel to something so that it's vertical, and cut a nock to comfortably fit the bowstring (Figure H). Sharpen the dowel with a pencil sharpener.

C. SPLIT THE FLETCHING

Fletchings stabilize the flight of the arrow and are traditionally made from feathers. We used chicken and cockatoo feathers, but turkey feathers are best. Using scissors or a trimming knife, halve the feathers lengthwise down the center of the quill, then trim to about 3" long.

Each half-feather has a natural cup that imparts spin to the arrow. Use fletches that are cupped in the same direction to provide a slight rotation that improves accuracy.

D. ATTACH THE FLETCHES

Using sticky tape to temporarily hold it in place, attach the first fletch at 90° to the nock (Figure I). Wrap the cotton thread around the shaft at the top end of the fletch to position it, then attach the second fletch $1/3$ of the way around, and the last one $2/3$ around.

Check positioning to ensure that the fletches all face the same way and are evenly spaced. Wrap the twine around the shaft, covering the front edges of the fletching. Then tie down the back ends of the fletches in the same way (Figure J).

E. TRIM AND GLUE

Put a few drops of varnish onto the twine to bind it firmly, and trim off any excess bits of twine and feather. You can use contact glue to press down the length of each fletch, but this isn't necessary.

3. MAKE THE TARGET AND SHOOT!

Paint a target, the bigger the better, on a piece of cardboard (Figure K), styrofoam, or a straw bale with paper pinned to it. Hang it and start shooting!

➕ Knot-tying techniques and more resources can be found at craftzine.com/07/play.

BAZAAR

CRAFTY GOODS WE ADORE. *Compiled by Natalie Zee Drieu*

Martha Stewart Crepe Paper Flower Kits

$13–$18

marthastewartcrafts.com

Having flowers around the house all the time is great, but as we all know, real flowers can get expensive! The crepe paper kits from Martha Stewart are a great way to give any room that extra splash of color, without breaking the bank and, of course, without wilted petals or dead blooms. Each kit comes with everything you need to create bright, beautiful crepe paper flowers. You can choose from a variety of blooms such as peonies, dogwood blossoms, daffodils, and tulips (pictured above).

Therapi Jade Yarn >>

soysilk.com

Jade isn't just for jewelry anymore, it's now yarn! This spring, South West Trading Company introduces a new line of jade yarn called Therapi, a blend of 50% fine wool, 20% silk, and 30% Bowlder, a crushed jadeite-based fiber. The yarn is soft, luxurious, and comes in 16 vibrant colors with a beautiful sheen.

Nantaka Joy "Things to Note" Dot Notebook

$13

nantakajoy.com

Created by Joy Deangdeelert Cho, Nantaka Joy's line of paper goods is pure decadence. With its signature scalloped right edge and colorful dot pattern in muted tones, it's beautiful. This small, lightweight journal has lots of writing room, yet still fits perfectly in a handbag. It's a guaranteed compliment every time I take it out to jot down a quick note.

Design-A-Doll

$60

ticcheandbea.com

Design-A-Doll by Ticche and Bea is a fun and easy doll project to make. I find it very satisfying to start something and finish it reasonably quickly, knowing that no one has the same exact doll as me. The kit comes with a great beginner's sewing set as well as a very helpful demo DVD. It's especially great for children, but also good for beginning or experienced crafters who just want to make something fun.

—Lindsey North

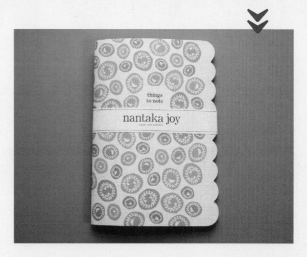

Pretty Pantry Gifts

By Tara Duggan $20
chroniclebooks.com

Package your jams, sauces, and pickles with the
Pretty Pantry Gifts kit. The box set comes with all
kinds of goodies you need to start your own delicious
jam-gifting, including a 48-page booklet filled with
15 recipes, as well as gift tags, labels, stickers, cello-
phane bags, and decorative fabric jar-toppers. It helps
make a great homemade gift for friends and family!

Craft Leftovers Monthly

$15/month
craftleftovers.com

Kristin Roach started the Craft Leftovers blog as a way to create
weekly projects that would force her to reclaim her stash of unused
yarn and scrap fabric. Two years later, it's a popular craft staple.
Now she's continuing her recycling movement with Craft Leftovers
Monthly, a subscription package that includes a 10-page zine, a
craft project, cutout project cards, and reclaimed leftovers such
as vintage fabric, buttons, iron-on patches, ribbon, and more. You
can purchase just one month of CL Monthly or subscribe for up to
three months.

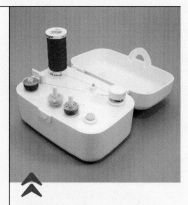

SideWinder Portable Bobbin Winder

$30
wrights.com

**Never again do you have to deal
with the hassle of unthreading and
rethreading your sewing machine
just to get a tiny bobbin wound for
your sewing or quilting project.**

**Now with my new favorite gadget,
the SideWinder, you can wind up all
the bobbins you need in a jiffy! With
its compact size, you can park it next
to your sewing machine, or drop it
into your tote bag to take to sewing
class. The SideWinder works with
most bobbin types, so check online
to find out if yours are compatible.**

BUSINESS REPLY MAIL

FIRST-CLASS MAIL   PERMIT NO 865   NORTH HOLLYWOOD CA

POSTAGE WILL BE PAID BY ADDRESSEE

Craft:

PO BOX 17046
NORTH HOLLYWOOD CA 91615-9588

BUSINESS REPLY MAIL

FIRST-CLASS MAIL   PERMIT NO 865   NORTH HOLLYWOOD CA

POSTAGE WILL BE PAID BY ADDRESSEE

Craft:

PO BOX 17046
NORTH HOLLYWOOD CA 91615-9588

CRAFT LOOKS AT BOOKS

❮❮ 49 Sensational Skirts

By Alison Willoughby Interweave Press **$25**
interweave.com

One of my goals this year is to make more clothing, and *49 Sensational Skirts* by U.K. textile designer Alison Willoughby could easily help me expand my wardrobe while learning how to create one-of-a-kind designs. The book is filled with beautiful skirts embellished with techniques such as layering, appliqué, embroidery, ruching, pleating, and even fabric printing! Novice sewers needn't worry, Willoughby also brings in core sewing techniques so you can learn how to sew while you pick up fashion design skills along the way.

❮❮ Bead Simple

By Susan Beal Taunton Press **$20**
taunton.com

A bead store opened up in my hometown when I was in ninth grade, and I had a brief love affair with beading. For years afterward, even a glimpse of a bead store made me wince at the memory. Then I got hold of a copy of Susan Beal's *Bead Simple*, and got that flutter again. The photographs are gorgeous, the instructions are as clear as day, and there are a ton of projects that I'd actually want to make. Even better, you get the feeling that everything, from vintage buttons to stuff from the hardware store, can be a bead. —Arwen O'Reilly

❮❮ Alabama Stitch Book

By Natalie Chanin with Stacie Stukin Harry N. Abrams, Inc. **$35**
hnabooks.com

Filled with exquisite photos of beautiful projects set amidst Alabama landscapes, the *Alabama Stitch Book* blew me away. Chanin not only teaches us her special appliqué and stitching techniques, but also gives us a glimpse inside her design process. My favorite technique is the reverse appliqué, beautifully applied to skirts, clothing, and table-cloths throughout the book. Patterns and stencils are also included.

❮❮ Warm Fuzzies

By Betz White F+W Publications **$23**
fwbookstore.com

I've been in love with the crafts of Betz White since I laid eyes on her felted cupcake pincushions. Who could believe such cuteness was made from old sweaters? With her new book, *Warm Fuzzies*, White brings us 30 adorable projects made with recycled felted sweaters, including pillows, hats, journal covers, and of course cupcakes. You'll find yourself wanting to make more and more cuteness.

Add some moody light to the dark spots in your life with these hanging votives. They look great outdoors (the globe keeps the wind from blowing out the flame) and nice indoors, too (who doesn't like hanging candles?), and if you can squeeze a pair of needlenose pliers and string a bead, you're almost there.

You will need: 6" clear glass ceiling light fixture globes, Soft Flex nylon-coated stainless steel beading wire (0.019" diameter), crimp beads, needlenose pliers, glass beads, sand, glass votives, candles

1. Cut and crimp.

Cut 2 pieces of beading wire, each at twice the total length that you want the globe to hang, plus 5". Hold them together, and slide a crimp bead down to a spot about 2½" above the midpoint of the strands. Crimp into place, add 2 more, and crimp those too. Now, starting from the other end of the beading wires, slide a crimp bead to a spot about 6" from the first 3.

2. Secure.

Part the beading wires between the loose bead and the first 3, and wrap them around the lip of the globe. Slide the loose bead down against the globe so that the wire hugs the narrow underside of its lip (like tightening a necktie), and crimp in place. Add 2 more behind it, and crimp those too. The globe should be securely supported with the wire rigging.

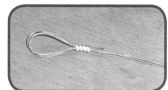

3. String.

String the glass beads over both wires in each pair, beading the entire length of each, stopping about 3" short of the ends.

4. Loop.

Slide 4 large crimp beads over all 4 ends of the wire, and loop the wires by bringing them back through the crimp beads. Squeeze the crimp beads firmly with pliers.

5. Glow.

Fill the globe about 1½" deep with sand or gravel, position the votive, hang the globe, and spark it up.

Photography by Matt Maranian

Matt Maranian is a designer and best-selling author who lives in Brattleboro, Vt.

Cathy Callahan
Old School

» Cathy Callahan is a crafter and window dresser who draws inspiration from vintage crafts. She blogs about 60s and 70s crafts at cathyofcalifornia.typepad.com.

Cut-and-Clip Decor

Brightly colored felt flowers add a splash of panache.

One of the ways that people in the counterculture of the 60s symbolized rebellion was to decorate or personalize their clothing. The rules pertaining to traditional craft techniques like embroidery, stitchery, and needlepoint were being broken. Just think of the amazing jackets Jimi Hendrix used to wear.

What was a political statement in the 60s became fun and playful by the time it hit the mainstream in the 70s. And since crafts and home sewing were so popular at the time, it seemed that everyone was in on the act. I made my own denim bib overalls in my junior high sewing class and then embellished them with a turtle appliqué.

Even if you weren't very crafty, you could always simply sew on a patch that you purchased at the fabric store. And, of course, inspiration could be found in just about any craft magazine.

I found the most adorable project in my copy of *Cut and Glue Décor*, a felt and foam how-to booklet from 1973. It was a pair of lime green vinyl clogs (with cork soles, no less) decorated with felt flowers. You simply cut the flowers out of felt with the patterns provided and then glued them on the shoe.

Inspiration could be found in just about any craft magazine in the 70s.

I thought it was a cute idea, but wouldn't the felt get dirty quickly? What if you grew tired of the decor that was now permanently glued to your shoe? Why not attach the flowers to clips for more versatility?

Here's my version that adds a little color to these neutral espadrilles. You could also attach just about any other little crafty item (maybe a yarn flower or a cluster of pompoms) to the clips. ✂

MATERIALS AND STEPS

Felt Wool felt works best. Use your favorite colors.
Your design Create your own or use the pattern provided at craftzine.com/07/oldschool.
Shoe clips (2) available at jewelry suppliers such as bergerbeads.net
Needle and thread
Craft glue

- - - - - - - - - - - - - - - -

1. Trace the pattern and cut out the felt.
2. Figure out the best position of the clip, where the flower will look best.
3. Stitch the clip to the underside of the larger flower.
4. Glue the smaller flower and its center on top of the larger flower; glue the leaves on the underside.
5. Allow glue to dry thoroughly before wearing.

Diana Baker
Recycle It

» Diane Baker lives, works, repurposes, and crafts with her family and dog in the rain, in Seattle. She's launching a nifty product she co-invented to protect brushes: *brushdefender.com*.

The Other Life of Umbrellas

Rain gear for the rest of our belongings.

Here in Seattle where the rain seems never to cease, getting outside keeps my mind, body, and mood in working order. Staying dry is a perennial concern, so I have plenty of rain gear to protect my body — but what about all my stuff? I've got my backpack, laptop, telephone, iPod, and PDA. As we all know, water does not mix well with paper or electronics.

Though my poncho or raincoat can protect my purse, backpack, and laptop, the resultant look is that of a lumpy packhorse out on the trail. The shelter that umbrellas provide should keep my things dry, but it doesn't. When the rain goes sideways, it drips down your back, and umbrellas have to be put up and down constantly. Plus, Seattleites don't look kindly upon umbrella users.

Because umbrellas typically malfunction and break, there's never a shortage of them to remake into something actually serviceable. Here are a few ideas to refashion your disused ones.

A

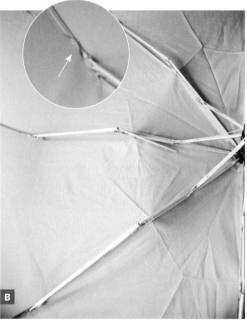

B

DECONSTRUCT AN UMBRELLA

1. Start by taking your umbrellas apart. Common long umbrellas and smaller folding umbrellas usually have an end that screws off. The nicest long umbrellas are more challenging; they have a metal ferrule riveted over the open cap. The easiest way to get this off is to wedge a small nail just under the edge, tap it under the metal with a hammer, and use it as a pry bar. You'll dig into the wood, but not much. When it's loosened up, you can finish it off with a pair of pliers (Figure A), then just pull the rivet out. (Be sure to protect your eyes in the process.)

2. When the open cap is removed, detach the canopy from the frame by slipping the tips off the ribs or cutting the threads if they're sewn on. First cut the threads that hold the canopy to the tips and the frame (Figure B), then cut off the tips.

3. Since the canopy is already a finished piece and just about the right size, all you need to do is patch the hole in the middle with duct tape or tent repair tape, available at any camping goods store. You're now ready to start making rain gear.

Photography by Diana Baker and Sam Murphy (B, E)

MAKE A BACKPACK COVER

1. The easiest no-sew project is the backpack cover. For this, think turtle shell. Take thick elastic cord and make a channel around the perimeter of the canopy by turning in a hem (Figure C). Sew it or secure it with duct tape, tent repair tape, or a glue-stitch product like Liquid Stitch. I don't recommend using seaming products that require heat, since umbrella fabric can melt easily. If you use tape to make the channel, you don't have to make it a solid seam; 2 or 3 pieces per panel works well, folding under the excess fabric at the angles. If the canopy is too big for your pack, make the channel bigger to make the canopy smaller.

2. Create your entry/exit point for the cord. This can be at the opposite side from the long tab that hangs off the umbrella for holding the furled canopy in place. On the inside of the canopy, fix a square of duct tape or tent repair tape on the channel. Snip a small slit in the square, being careful not to cut the outer fabric. Slip the cord through this slit and into the channel, then thread it around the perimeter and out the slit again (Figure D).

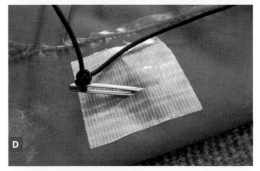

3. Experiment with the cord length, making it long enough to fit snugly around the backpack, but loose enough to slip on and off easily. Slip the ends of the elastic cord through a cord lock (available at fabric, camping, and craft stores). You can tie buttons to the cord ends as an attractive finish that also keeps the elastic from slipping out of the cord lock.

4. Slip your turtle shell over the backpack. Fasten the umbrella tab around one or both straps and snap it, or use velcro fasteners to hold the shell in place. It looks a bit like a giant shower cap, and works just as well to keep things dry (Figure E).

MAKE A LAPTOP PONCHO

1. To make a poncho cover for your portable computer or briefcase, detach the umbrella canopy and smooth out the center.

2. Overlap several pieces of duct tape or tent repair tape over the center, forming a rectangle about 2" wide and up to 6" long (Figure F). Or for a more finished look, follow these steps, substituting sewn and hemmed edges for the tape.

3. Based on the handle you want this to fit over, cut a centered slit or a rectangle out of the taped area (Figure G). The umbrella canopy will cover the case like a little poncho or parachute (Figure H). If there's a gap beneath the handle wide enough to let rain in, use dots of velcro to close it up.

4. You can also use the same premise to recycle your umbrella into a personal poncho, making the slit large enough for your head to go through.

NOTE: Another tactic is to open a seam between 2 panels, and finish both sides with either tape or seam adhesive, making your umbrella into a customized rain shawl. You can even wear it in a cowl arrangement by adding velcro, a snap, or a hook and eye.

MAKE A DRAWSTRING BAG

1. For all the rest of your stuff, you can turn your umbrella into a drawstring bag. Make this just like the turtle shell cover, but with regular cord, not elastic. Any cord will do for the closure, though it can't function as the handle unless you also sew the channel to make it sturdy.

2. You can use the bag without a handle by slipping your purse or shopping bag into it, drawing up the cord, and using the existing handle. Or add a strap, recycled from an old belt or a shoulder strap from a duffel (Figure I).

RECYCLE THE REMAINDERS

1. On long umbrellas, the wooden cane is a wonderful gardening tool for fruit picking. Snag a branch with the crook, and harvest or cut. I also use the cane for pulling blackberries close without slicing myself up on the prickly vines.

2. The metal skeleton of a reused umbrella is perfect as a drying rack for sweaters and socks, as long as you're careful not to snag them on the ends. It can also be used as stakes for vine plants like tomatoes. ✕

Wendy Tremayne
Re: Fitted

» Wendy Tremayne (gaiatreehouse.com) is renovating an RV park into a 100% reuse, off-grid B&B in Truth or Consequences, N.M. Another project, Swap-O-Rama-Rama (swaporamarama.org), is a clothing swap and DIY workshop designed to offer people an alternative to consumerism.

Journey of the *Yosegire* Quilt

An ancient technique makes its way around the globe.

Heather Cameron apologizes. Her spectacular patchwork quilt was not composed entirely from objects in roadside dumpsters — she supplemented with secondhand clothing from Swap-O-Rama-Rama, a semiannual event she produces in Vancouver, British Columbia, where she lives.

A seasoned reuse artist, Cameron often challenges her own high standards. Her intention for this project was not just to re-create a historical work in modern form, she wanted to experience the process of the patchwork quilters who inspired her.

Cameron was inspired by the Japanese quilting method *yosegire*, which means "to sew together." As a patchwork style, yosegire originated in the 16th century, but the premise of using scrap-made garments of seamed-together bits dates back long before that. Legend has it that the Buddha, who lived in the 6th century B.C., instructed his followers to wear patchwork garments patterned like the rice fields of India, assembled from discarded rags. The idea resonates with Buddhist teachings about the interconnectedness of all beings.

Cameron compares the history of the yosegire to the work of the women of Gee's Bend, Ala. Living below poverty level in an isolated African-American hamlet, these women craft scraps into ornate, abstract quilts. Necessity opens a portal from which unbounded and organic, fresh designs emerge.

"I'm drawn to the abject, the discarded, and the idea of restoration and redemption," Cameron says. "The Buddhist concept of yosegire exemplifies making something out of nothing, while the quilters of Gee's Bend work with what's too worn to be used anymore."

Cameron decided to take advantage of Vancouver's 2007 garbage strike and the growing piles of trash that lined her street. She gathered whatever clothing crossed her path, opting for those that were, for the upper classes, the least appealing — polyester stretch pants, an XL black lace negligee, and a chef's apron — as textiles that symbolize a range of labor and class. She also used pieces from her Swap-O-Rama-Rama.

After laundering and cutting out stains, Cameron innovated ways to combine different textiles such as knits and weaves. The project became a field of color and texture. One might liken it to the Buddha's vision of the fields of India, though Cameron, colored by the culture of her modern time, observes that her field resembles licorice allsorts candy.

Cameron believes in the living thread she participates in, one of nondifferentiation of the self and other, of opening one's consciousness to all the world. As the Sufi sage Hazrat Inayat Khan aptly said, "Liking comes from knowledge and dislike from ignorance."

MATERIALS

- » **SCAVENGED CLOTHING**
- » **BACKING FABRIC** OLD SHEETS ARE IDEAL.
- » **BATTING** SUCH AS AN OLD FLANNEL SHEET
- » **CUTTING MAT**
- » **ROTARY CUTTER**
- » **ACRYLIC RULER**
- » **THREAD**
- » **SCISSORS**
- » **SAFETY PINS**
- » **SEWING MACHINE**

Photography by Heather Cameron

PATCHWORK QUILT FROM CLOTHING SCRAPS

1. Find and cut clothes.
Trim unusable areas, but keep the interesting elements such as buttons or pockets. Use the rotary cutter, mat, and acrylic ruler to cut garments into even strips (Figure A). For a quick tutorial, see purlbee.com/rotary-cutter-tutorial.

2. Sew strips together.
For the nucleus of the quilt, randomly grab a handful of strips, join them end to end with a ¼" seam, then press the fabric (Figure B). For an angled seam, lay 2 strips face up, overlap the ends, and use the rotary cutter to cut both layers at once. This makes for accurate joins. Varying your seam angles makes for a lively patchwork. Repeat until you've sewn strips the length of your quilt. When you have multiple full-length strips, begin sewing them together (Figure C).

3. Assemble the quilt.
Place the pieces in this order, making a "sandwich": backing layer facedown, batting layer, then top layer face up (Figure D). Make sure all layers lie smooth, then secure them in place with safety pins.

4. Sew the quilt.
"Stitch in the ditch" sewing is recommended for this project — stitches straight down the seams of the patchwork. Keep your presser foot aligned right on top of the seam, and try to have the needle enter the fabric on the low side of the seam. Trim the edges straight. Stitch or zigzag around the edge of the quilt. For the binding, cut 1⅜" bias strips with the rotary cutter. Attach bias to the edge of the reverse side of the quilt using a ¼" seam (Figure E).

5. Clean and prepare for display.
Launder the quilt in the washing machine set to "cold" and if possible, "gentle." Then toss it in the dryer, also set to "gentle" or "low." On display, your stunning quilt will look both vintage and fresh (Figure F). ✄

➕ More of Heather Cameron's work can be seen at truestitches.blogspot.com.

Heather Cameron just came back from her dream vacation of a lifetime in Japan with way too many old Kimonos.

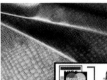

Art
BerkleyIllustration $7

Jewelry
jascamille

Ceramics & Pottery
DagaDesign $16

Jewelry
AlmaB $20

Paper Goods
Squeedles $3

Accessories
terrygraziano

Bags & Purses
Reiter8 $55

Needlecraft
Ottoman $30

Jewelry
applecreekdesigns $18

Children
HoldTheFlour

Jewelry
AnthroPoMorphCo $7.25

Bags & Purses
Tributary $15

Bath & Beauty
Naiad $5

Jewelry
BabyJewlz

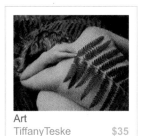

Art
TiffanyTeske $35

Jewelry
jennlyn54 $129

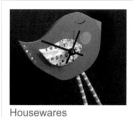

Housewares
Reincarnations $28

Patterns
AngelaCatirina

Discover these unique creations and more, with over 1,300,000 handmade goods and supplies for s
on Etsy. To find any of the items above, each in their own shop, go to: www.shopname.etsy.com

iture
eball $45

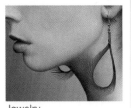

Jewelry
neawear $22

Etsy.com

Your place to buy and
sell all things handmade™

rything Else
raJewelry $21

Needlecraft
christinaward $30

Supplies
ViragoCreations $9.95

Needlecraft
lagreen $12

elry
lle $245

Accessories
shopwhimsy $12

Bags & Purses
sarahjanedesigns $50

Jewelry
tinarice $35

s
keyblues $18

Art
JenniferSquires $45

Jewelry
ennadesign $22

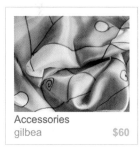

Accessories
gilbea $60

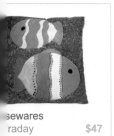

sewares
raday $47

Jewelry
glennacarlton $200

Quilts
babyannequilts $220

Supplies
kittygrrlz $35

Buy Handmade

Shining Through

This enchanted dresser has come a long way since it was tossed into an alley on trash day. When **Angelique Bamberg** rescued it over a year ago, "it was in pretty rough condition," covered in dings and an ugly layer of alligatored varnish. Bamberg's first idea was to simply cover the dresser in a coat of paint. But once she removed the varnish, she was surprised at the beauty she found underneath. "The problem was that the veneer was too dinged up to be refinished, but too pretty to cover up."

Trained as a historic preservationist, this Pittsburg, Penn. resident came up with a brilliant solution: cover most of the dresser in paint while masking off a tree shape in the front to allow some of the lovely wood to shine through.

Though Bamberg had stenciled before (including a pattern of skeleton keys on the walls of her 100-year-old fixer-upper), using painter's tape to mask the tree was problematic: "When I peeled it off after painting, I found that the primer had seeped under the edges, blurring the entire design." It took many hours with a razor blade to restore a crisp outline.

The dresser now brightens up her 3-year-old daughter's room. "I like the idea of her having things that are unique and handmade just for her," says Bamberg. "I also like to think that seeing me work on pieces like this will give her an appreciation for the creative potential of things that others might just throw away."

—Carla Sinclair

Photograph by Brian Kaldorf